THE EIGHTH STAGE OF FANDOM

THE EIGHTH STAGE OF FANDOM

ROBERT BLOCH

Introduction by Wilson Tucker

Special Afterword by Harlan Ellison

The Wildside Press

THE EIGHTH STAGE OF FANDOM

Special thanks to Lynn Crosson and Alice Moskow for help in typesetting this book.

"The Seven Ages of Fan," from *The Fanscient* #6, Winter 1949. "Gafia House," from *Hyphen* #21, October, 1958."Poe and Me," from *Vanations* #6, July, 1953. "Left at The Post," from *Slant* #7, Winter, 1952-53. "Credo for Fantasy Writers," from *Peon*, 2nd Annish, 1950. "Immodest Proposal," from *New Purpose*, January 1, 1949. "The Birth of a Notion," from *The Zed*, March, 1955. "A Letter from Sally Ann Bloch," from *Femizine* #5, February, 1955. "McGuffey's First Science Fiction Reader," from *Fandora's Box* copyright © 1957 by Greenleaf Publishing Company for *Imagination*, April, 1957. "The Tape of Things to Come," from *Oopsla!* #9, January, 1953. "Bah! Humbug!" from *Oopsla!* #25, July, 1958. "I'll Fry Tomorrow," from *Science Fiction Five-Yearly* #1, November-December, 1956. "Forty Whacks," from *Excelsior* #2, April, 1957. "Through a Picture-Tube, Darkly," from *The Vinegar Worm* #3, Fall, 1957. "In Memoriam: W.T.," from *Isomer* #2, September 27, 1955. "Lost and Found Department," from *Hodge-Podge* #10, July-August, 1954. "The Demolished Fan," from *Oopsla!*, January, 1954. "A Way of Life," from "Fandora's Box," copyright © 1956, 1957 by Greenleaf Publishing Company for *Imagination*, December, 1956, August, 1956; August, 1957. "Every Man His Own Psychiatrist," from *New Purposes* #12, June 15, 1949. "This Method of Catharsis," from *The Acolyte*, Fall, 1945. "Them Ain't Bongo Drums — That's Opportunity Knocking!" from *Shangri-L'Affaires* #39, October, 1958. "Children of Blunder," from *Grue* #27, February, 1956. "How Weak Was My End," from *Quandry*, June, 1952. "How to Attend a Science Fiction Convention," from *Fan Warp* #1, 1953. "Exerpts from a Letter to P. Howard Lyons," from *Canadian Fandom*, December, 1954. "Pro and Con," from *Bem* #3, September, 1954. "At the Headwaters," from *Kteic Magazine* #29, October,1955. "Letter to a Convention-Goer," from *Newyorcon Program Book*, September, 1956. "Surrogate in '58," from *Oopsla!* #23, November, 1957. "The Incredible Head-Shrinking Man," from *Sigbo* #5, 1958. "Pete Kelly's Blue Dragnet," from *Gasp!* #7, January, 1956."The Ealing Art," from *Hyphen* #18, May, 1957. "The Past Recaptured," from *Science Fiction Fifty Yearly* #1, November, 1957. "Doctor Bloomington, I Presume?" from *Science Fiction Fifty Yearly* #1, November, 1957. "The Fabulous Mr. Tucker," from *Masque*, 19??. "The Art of William Rotsler," from *Innuendo*, August,1958. "Willis in America," from *Hyphen* #3, February, 1953. "Second Coming!" from *New Purposes* #9, May 1, 1949. "A Public Apology," from *New Purposes* #16, March, 1950. "Worst Foot Forward," from *Inside* #15, May, 1956. "Just a Goddamn Hobby," from *Psychotic* #20, May-June-July, 1955. "The Communist," from *Destiny* #10, Summer, 1954. "The Dead-Beat Generation" was written for *Grue*. "Cause to Read Joyce," from *Hyphen* #12, December, 1954. "From Hubbub Horizontal," from *Nandu* #13, March, 1956. "The Lomokome Papers," from *Stf-in-Gen & Bolide (Sigbo)* #3, 1957. "A Non-Lewis Carol," from *Psychotic* #19, March-April, 1955. "Cassandra," from *Vega* #10, August, 1953. "Jabberwocky for Fandom," from *Rea* #2, Fall, 1954.

CONTENTS

To

That Sterling Neo-Fan

EDWARD E. SMITH, Ph.D.

with an affection I am sure is
shared by all who have ever been
privileged to know him

BLOCH IS SUPERB

I said this about Robert Bloch twenty-nine years ago when writing the introduction to the 1962 edition of this volume:

"Introduce Robert Bloch? Yes, of course. You have to ask?

"He has been happily wallowing in the same rut since his first fan efforts appeared in *The Fantasy Fan* and *Marvel Tales* in 1934. Surely you've noticed that — there is no escaping this fantastic flood of words found in every fan journal published today. (Once, some years ago, a magazine appeared in Arizona that promised *not* to print a Bloch piece for a period of five years. Its editor was immediately swamped with cash subscriptions. Unfortunately the money went to the editor's head and he absconded.)"

Unhappily, that fantastic flood of words in the fan journals has dried up, and Bloch foresaw it happening in his Preface to the 1962 edition. He said: "It may well be that I won't write very many more items for amateur publication in the future. I don't have the endurance I used to and neither, I suspect, do the readers. But it has been fun — and underneath the insults and invective, I hope it's possible to detect the very real warmth and affection I feel for the field and the people therein."

A hundred fan editors, at least, and a thousand readers, at least, regret that the forecast came true. You will know why after you have read the contents of this book. Bloch wrote of wondrous things, of fans and foibles and fanzines, of science fiction and the outer world, all with wit and elegance. He wrote often with tongue in cheek and he often carried sharp pins to puncture egos larger than great balloons. Oh, how we need that wit and those pins today!

And again, paraphrasing that introduction of 1962, I repeat this:

Robert Bloch has two sides which have created parallel ruts. This opposite and equal side is his professional facet, and if my research is accurate he also sold his first story to *Weird Tales* in 1934. Many more such sales followed and *Weird Tales* is still with us today despite his presence. Possibly because of his presence, for he *is* a decent writer, you know. He once collaborated with Edgar Allan Poe, and after that collaboration was published Poe was not heard to complain.

Running or wallowing in his professional rut, Bloch has produced memorable prose: have you read "The Cloak" and "The Shoes" in *Unknown*; have you read "The Opener of the Way" in *Weird Tales*; do you remember "The Strange Flight of Richard Clayton" in *Amazing Stories*? He wrote my favorite fantasy, "The Movie People," and he also wrote a book that made Alfred Hitchcock famous. I suspect that he is thoroughly tired of blurbs that now read, "By the author of *Psycho*."

Bloch has had the singular fate of watching one short story, "Yours Truly, Jack the Ripper," appear in print more often than a political promise to impose no new taxes. That story was reprinted once again in September 1991 in a volume called *Fantastic Chicago*, the souvenir book of the Chicago World Science Fiction Convention. There is no truth to the rumor that it will appear one more time next year in a trade publication called *Guide to Approved Mortuaries*, edited by Burke and Hare.

The other rut, his fannish rut, is partially in evidence in this volume. Only an encyclopedia publisher with the gall to charge an enormous fee could afford to bring out the complete Robert Bloch, but until that bright day comes along this volume will do. I would particularly recommend "Bah! Humbug!" to your attention, along with "Poe and Me" and "The Lomokome Papers" (sometimes called "The Locomotive Papers") as fair samples of the many moods of the man. I've known him personally for forty-five years but it is still difficult to say which I treasure most: the many letters from him, the fanzine articles represented in this volume, or the infrequent times we have spent together at one convention or another. Together, we were banned from the TV airwaves in Louisville, Kentucky, and I treasure that memory. Together, we failed to explore Mammoth Cave in Kentucky, and I don't know if I treasure that memory. Together, we explored the wonders of Niagara Falls but Robert Bloch may not care to recall that memory — by accident we had booked into a honeymoon motel.

Physically he is tall and thin, rather dark or tanned, and possessed of a diabolical sense of humor. It has often been said that he has the heart of a small boy, which he keeps in a jar on his desk. That image of a desk cannot be pushed too far. He would not want to admit that he has been found with his foot in a drawer and his fingers in the till. His wife Elly suffers him patiently, and I have often wondered how she manages that.

It is *not* true that he likes his admirers to stand up and cheer when he enters the room. He is a modest man. But we frequently cheer when he stops speaking. We stand and applaud too, for Bloch is superb.

With affection,

Wilson Tucker
Bloomington, Ill.
October 8, 1991

PREFACE

A professional writer is a man who writes for money and believes that only an idiot gives away his work for nothing.

Shake hands with an idiot.

But before you send for the little men with the restraint-jackets (and when you do, I take a size 16, no starch in the collars, please) let me say that I've enjoyed turning out the pieces I've done gratis for science fiction fan magazines.

When Earl Kemp suggested I help him assemble a collection of such material, I discovered to my horror (and quite possibly, to yours) that there were several hundred to choose from during the past twenty-five years. The most that can be said for this selection is that it's fairly representative.

Omitted were many earlier efforts, topical in their time, but probably incomprehensible to today's reader. ("Today's reader" being a man whose TV set is temporarily out of order.) Some of the recognizably dated items which were included deal with matters I trust are still pertinent. For example, "Worst Foot Forward" concerns the science fiction boom-and-bust cycle of 1950-54 — but this same cycle repeated itself in 1955-59, and for what I believe to be the same reasons. "The Communist" was written during the height of the Red Scare, and there are other souvenirs of past uproars — both in our own little microcosm of fandom and in the great unreal world outside.

It may well be that I won't write very many more items for amateur publication in the future. I don't have the endurance I used to and neither, I suspect, do the readers. But it has been fun — and underneath the insults and invective, I hope it's possible to detect the very real warmth and affection I feel for the field and the people therein.

One final word of explanation. I was hoping to contribute an appendix to this book, but my doctor refused to operate.

ROBERT BLOCH
Studio City, California
August 31, 1962

THE SEVEN AGES OF FAN

One of the occupational hazards of fantasy writing (along with ulcers, fights with the loan companies and schizophrenia) is a constant exposure to fandom.

For years I have kept silent on the subject (far be it from me to bite the hand that feeds me, however poorly) but there comes a time when truth cries out for utterance. Only last night, the time came to me. I was sitting at the fire, nodding away as is my wont when listening to my wife, when a strange veiled figure entered the room.

"Utterance!" it yelled. "Utterance!"

"Who, pray," I enquired politely, "the hell are you?"

"I am Truth," replied the veiled figure, "and I am crying out for Utterance, who couldn't make it tonight and besides which he has a sore throat."

"That is very interesting," I mused, ripping the veil aside and discovering the figure of my daughter. "And now if you will kindly scram outta here I will get down to my business, which is to write an article about the Seven Ages of Fan."

It was, and is, my purpose to discuss the strange metamorphosis which seems to take place in the character, personality, aims and attitudes of the Average Fan as I have observed him thru the years, darkly.

This survey has absolutely nothing in common with Shakespeare's "Seven Ages of Man" except, perhaps, that Shakespeare and myself are both writers.

End of digression. To work, to wit:

THE FIRST AGE OF FAN

is the Quiescent, or reader-interest age. During this brief period our embryonic fan buys several fantasy magazines, weird or sf, and proceeds to actually read them from cover to cover. I know that some of the more blasé and sophisticated fans are going to dispute this fact, but I can vouch for it — I have actually seen it happen with my own eyes. In the first stage, I maintain, fans really read the magazines.

THE SECOND AGE OF FAN

follows, alas, all too quickly upon the heels of the initial period. This is the Chirospastic stage, characterized by Writer's Cramp, during which the neophyte fan begins to write letters to the pro magazines commenting on the stories and urging that the editors throw out everything except Kuttner yarns.

THE THIRD AGE OF FAN

finds the now enthralled victim sending personal letters c/o the editors to his favorite authors (outside of Kuttner, most fans seem to like Lewis Padgett, Keith Hammond, Lawrence O'Donnell, Will Garth, Hudson Hastings, Paul Edmonds and such people). These letters consist of requests for autographs, favorable comments on published writings and a solicitation that the author read the fan's writings and revise them or collaborate with him on stories.

THE FOURTH AGE OF FAN

represents a crucial phase in his development. It is characterized by a chance exposure to a fan magazine, followed quickly by high fever, delirium and spots before the eyes — the latter caused by the faulty mimeographing of the magazine. Usually, without pause or rallying, the patient goes directly into:

THE FIFTH AGE OF FAN

which consists of publishing his own fan magazine and ruthlessly spreading it over the entire fan world. By this time, of course, what with writing to editors and reading fan mags and writing to authors and writing fan mags, the fan has absolutely no time left to read any more pro magazines. And he wouldn't care for the stuff if he did read it. For he is now a full-fledged fan in mid career and by this time he is entering the sixth stage which is almost inevitably fatal.

THE SIXTH AGE OF FAN

is characterized by "joining-fever," sometimes known as sympathetic herd-delusion or mass-hysteria. In this state, the fan rushes out and meets other sufferers. He often organizes and not infrequently goes so far as to convene. Sometimes he even draws up and charters. Fans visit him. He visits fans. Before he knows it he has entered into personal or literary contact with dozens of others, and has at least eight bitter feuds going at the same time.

Once this stage is reached, there is no turning back. The rest is inevitable. There remains only —

THE SEVENTH AGE OF FAN

Tottering on the brink of the abyss, the fan presents a truly pitiable picture: a haggard caricature of what was once a healthy, happy 12-year-old boy. He cannot read the pro magazines anymore, because he and his fellow fans know that they stink. He cannot write to the editors any more, because they are his bitter enemies. He is all washed up with the pro authors who refused to collaborate with him on his epics. He no longer finds time to read even the fan mags; of course, he gets very few of these because his feuds have cut him off the mailing lists. As for his own fan mag, he doesn't bother to put it out — there is no one left to mail it to after he rules out all of those who disagree with him. And he has alienated his personal contacts due to long, bitter arguments over Shaver, *The World of Null-A* or Ghu-Ghu.

No, there is no way to retrace his steps. He can only take the plunge, over the edge of the precipice. He has reached the SEVENTH STAGE. Hating fantasy fiction, fantasy readers, fantasy editors, fantasy authors and fantasy fans, there is nothing left for him to do but become a fantasy publisher, which he does!

What more is there to say? The moral is all too obvious. If there are those among you who are in any of the preliminary phases, do not delude yourself.

Repent now, before it is too late. Turn back, I beseech you! Become an agent, become a pro author, become anything, however low and vile — but do it now, while there is yet time and hope.

But . . . if, in spite of all my pleas, warnings and entreaties . . . you succumb and reach that fatal, final SEVENTH STATE . . .

Then get in touch with me. I've got a lot of crud lying around, suitable for publication in book form. The line forms at your left.

GAFIA HOUSE

You have to have a pretty detailed map if you want to locate Weyauwega, Wisconsin.

Even on a highway map of the state, Weyauwega figures as a mere flyspeck. In fact I know of several drivers who set out for Weyauwega, drove a couple of hundred miles and actually finished up on a flyspeck instead.

To make it still further confusing, none of them could tell the difference.

But on the face of it (the map, that is) this little community could well qualify as Nowhere, U.S.A. The only way to reach it through public transportation is via Greyhound Bus, and nobody ever uses that except myself, and a few greyhounds.

So when the family and I moved up here about five years ago, we were pretty well resigned to the fact that we'd be living in an isolation booth, and the $64,000 question was whether or not we'd ever see anyone.

As a result, I didn't even bother to invest in a guest-book. Who was ever going to sign it? After all, Weyauwega wasn't a fannish stopping place. It boasts none of the attractions of gay, cosmopolitan Belfast, with its dissolute fleshpots, its corrupt police force, its depraved government officials and its notorious indoor sports. Nor is Weyauwega a cultural Mecca such as Bloomington, Illinois. It even lacks the exotic charm of Los Angeles, that rugged Western community where men are men, sometimes.

Not only did we not expect any visitors — we did our best to discourage them. To this end we purchased a vicious dog named Tiny, the product of a liaison between a Toy Manchester Terrier and a bubonic rat. Tiny (who spends her days on my lap and her nights in my wife's bed, and thus lends herself aptly to all sorts of innuendo) is a phenomenal creature in that she is equally deadly at both ends. One end boasts a formidable bark, which is discharged frequently. The other end, although silent, is no less frequent in its discharges. (I do not wish to malign the dog, however, she *is* housebroken, and quite effectively. Every morning she scratches at my bed for me to get up and let her out. One morning, as I hastily struggled into my bathrobe, the poor dog just couldn't wait — so she intelligently took aim and let go into my bedroom slipper.)

In addition, we happen to live on a street which had neither signposts nor house-numbers until last year. It seemed well nigh impossible that anyone would ever find us here, granted even that morbid curiosity would impel them to make the attempt.

And such proved to be the case. During the period of our residence in Weyauwega the only fans or pros ever to cross our threshold have been Dean Grennell and family, Curtis Janke, Stuart Hoffman, Ted Wagner, Rita Krohne, Raymond A. Palmer, Lynn Hickman, Richard S. Shaver, William Hamling and family, Ted and Judy Dikty, Bob Tucker and family, Bea and Pat Mahaffey, Martin Greenberg, Fritz Leiber, Boyd Raeburn, Ron Kidder, Gerald Stewart, Bob and Barbara Silverberg, Richard Eney, Roberta Gibson (née Collins), Rog Phillips, Evelyn Paige, Arthur and Phyllis Economou, Jack Speer (né John Bristol), William Grant and his mother, Andy and Jean Young and family and a couple of those door-to-door representatives who are always coming around trying to sign me up for the Cosmic Circle.

The most frequent visitor, of course, has been Grennell, who up until recently passed near town every third week on his sales route. He and the family often drive up during the summer months, in increasingly bigger cars. As a result, tapes have been made and played in the livingroom, and a mimeograph has disturbed the orderly array of bottles on the kitchen table.

The same kitchen table has served as a poker table for Tucker, and babies have been diapered on it — although not during the poker game, when we usually had a large pot.

Yes, the Great World has come to Weyauwega, bringing touches of color and glamour into our drab lives. Bob Silverberg (that Kleenex completist) enriched his collection with several pieces of toilet tissue. Roberta Gibson left, as a momento of her stay, a carved figurine of a Japanese maiden in her bath; Bill Grant's mother sent a landscape in oils which graces the livingroom; Evelyn Paige displayed her collection of 427 earrings (we never did find the missing 428th one); Fritz Leiber chopped down a tree. You haven't lived until you've heard Richard S. Shaver discuss deros in your very own parlor, watched the Canadians chasing rabbits across the field in their sports cars or awakened in the morning to find Bea and Pat Mahaffey doing the breakfast dishes for you.

The house is full of memories, now. Here is the place where Frances Hamling hornswoggled me into taking over "Pandora's Box" in *Imagination*; here is the chair Ted Dikty sat on (the one with the broken springs), and my wife's lap that Marty Greenberg sat on; here is a hair from Andy Young's beard; here is a hole in the carpet from the time Tucker spilled the Jim Beam; here is a hole in the floor from the time Lynn Hickman spilled the Jack Daniels.

There's no sense fighting it any longer; when spring comes, I'll probably call in the workmen and build a ghoodminton court.

But wait until I get my hands on that joker who said, "It is a proud and *lonely* thing to be a fan."

POE AND ME

The sf world was set back on its heels by one of the strangest writing combinations ever to sell a story. Separately the two collaborators are well-known and well-liked, but when they got together and wrote "The Lighthouse" for *Fantastic* . . . then it was something indeed. Never before had Robert Bloch and Edgar Allan Poe collaborated together. To bring you the inside truth . . . the story behind the story, I took the liberty of questioning Mr. Bloch in regard to it. My questions and his answers follow.

— Norman G. Browne

Q: In general, how did you like collaborating with Mr. Poe?

A: Fine. He didn't ask for a split on the check.

Q: Did you experience any trouble while collaborating with Mr. Poe?

A: Not as much as I usually have when I've attempted to work with other amateurs.

Q: During the collaboration, did you find Mr. Poe to be temperamental?

A: Quite the contrary. He was so quiet I scarcely knew he was around.

Q: Did Mr. Poe have any eccentricities?

A: Well, one thing . . . he kept looking over his shoulder and claiming he saw a raven. This was absurd.

Q: Do you think Mr. Poe found you eccentric in any way?

A: He seemed to. I kept looking over *my* shoulder and claiming I saw a black cat. He said that was absurd.

Q: Does Mr. Poe have any bad habits you found irritating?

A: Yes. He drinks Amontillado right out of the bottle.

Q: Do you have any bad habits that Mr. Poe found irritating?

A: Yes. I drink Amontillado right out of the cask.

Q: Was this the first time you had ever met Mr. Poe?

A: Heavens to Betsy, no! He and I met many years ago at the house of an oldtime fan named Usher.

Q: Did you take a liking to Mr. Poe?

A: Of course. The kid shows promise of developing into a real writer. A sort of Edgar Allan Pro.

Q: Do you think he took a liking to you?

A: Why not? I'm very lovable, really. Beneath these ragged trousers there beats a heart of gold.

Q: Did you use an orthodox method of collaboration . . . each writing a word of the story in alteration? Or did you use an unorthodox method, such as writing a sentence in turn?

A: We went further than that. We took turns writing each letter of each word. This got pretty tiresome, so along about the middle, he handled all the vowels and I handled the consonants. Then he complained of vowel trouble, so we took turns writing syllables.

Q: Is it true that Mr. Ziff of the Ziff-Davis Publications regards Mr. Poe as "Quite the up-and-coming young writer?"

A: Yes, but wait until he hears about Jules Verne!

Q: A vicious rumor has it that Mr. Poe wrote the first half of "The Lighthouse" and you wrote the last half. Would you care to make a statement commenting on this?

A: I actually wrote four-fifths of the story. Mr. Poe drank the other fifth.

Q: Is it true that you and Mr. Poe isolated yourselves in a lighthouse while writing the story?

A: This is an error, based on the fact that Mr. Poe and I shared the same quarters during our collaboration. What I actually said was that, "Mr. Poe and I have set up in a lighthousekeeping apartment together."

Q: In closing, are there any further statements you wish to make regarding Mr. Poe, yourself, and your collaboration?

A: It was a pleasant experience, but next time I'm going to collaborate with Kathleen Winsor!

LEFT AT THE POST

People are always asking me, "Bloch, what kind of mail does a professional writer get? What kind of mail does a professional writer get? What kind of—" And so forth. It's enough to drive me crazy.

So finally I decided to do something about it.

I went crazy.

Just to show you why, I'll give you a sample of my incoming correspondence for November 22nd. (If there are any smarties who protest that November 22nd is Thanksgiving Day this year and for this reason no mail is delivered, all I can say is that they belong over here in the states: I'd gladly trade places with them sight unseen, if only to get away from the postman's ring. It's a rather large ring with a fake diamond in it, and it hurts my eyes.)

So without further ado, I take you to the morning of November 22nd, and drop you there with a dull thud.

I sit down at my desk with the correspondence on one side of my typewriter and the wastebasket on the other. I contemplate the stack of letters and packages, then pick up a letter opener and run my finger along the edge. Sighing deeply as I realize it isn't quite sharp enough to cut my throat, I attack the mail.

Ah, a letter from Ireland — and not in Gaelic, either!

This I must read . . . I open it with breathless anticipation (also the letter-opener, which makes it easier) and what do I find?

A wretched scrawl from somebody named Willis, trying to cadge material for a fanzine. This goes in the wastebasket, just to line the bottom properly.

Then the inevitable dunning letters. One, two, three, four, five — I like to get bills, because I don't have to bother opening them. Into the basket. Makes a pretty pile, too.

And then, a thunderbolt. As I take up the next piece the horrid realization hits me.

Galaxy has folded!

Yes, folded. The postman must have sat on it (He must have been getting behind in his deliveries).

I unfold it and put it aside, then pick up a fanzine. It's from abroad. Something called *Slant*: one of those dry pedantic publications — but then, those chaps have no sense of humor, you know. I riffle the pages and check some of the more glaring errors and inaccuracies — for example, a pen sketch of Lee Hoffman which shows her as a *white* girl.

Clunk! It hits the basket as I pick up a letter from a prominent editor, begging me to do another novel under one of my pseudonyms — Robert A. Heinlein or A. E. van Vogt. I laugh heartily until the tears come to my eyes: then wipe them with a thousand dollar bill from my fine collection of Japanese war currency. A brief pencilled notation, advising the editor that from now on I will use only one pseudonym, Ray Bradbury, and the letter is filed away until the afternoon, at which time I shall write the novel.

Now, a "fan letter" from still another amateur editor. This requires special treatment. He had written asking for material in the past, and I begged off, telling him I was under doctor's orders not to do any more work. Whereupon he wrote back, "I don't believe you. What's supposed to be the matter?"

My answer was brief and to the point.

"Kidney trouble."

Again, his reply. "I don't believe you."

So I wrote, "Am sending you a specimen under separate cover."

Back came his letter. "Examined your specimen and you don't have kidney trouble at all."

To which I answered, "Are you positive?"

Answer, as of today: "No, but your specimen is!"

This bothers me, because all the time I thought I was sending him a negative answer . . .

Now a note from Forrest J Ackerman, who is starting a movement to introduce a branch of naval dianetics, in an effort to make it easier to clear the decks. This is filed, with other dianetics gags, in the standard memory bank or wastebasket.

And now, a flattering invitation from a learned scientist who has just read a lunar flight story of mine and is so impressed that he urges me to take a flying jump at the moon . . .

What's this? *Another* note from the Willis person, quote: "Hurry up with that article, I haven't got all day!"

Such persistence — always harping on something.

Clunk . . . into the basket.

An invitation to read one of my stories aloud at the annual banquet of the School for the Deaf . . . A solicitation for an international fund now being raised to scrape the guano off the white cliffs of Dover . . . and a whole series of requests for my autograph from various tradesmen who would like to see it on checks.

The wastebasket is almost full.

I reach down and scrabble around in it to test the depth, and then breathe a sigh of relief. My correspondence is at an end, and there is room. With a stern cry of "Rockets Awaaaay!" I slit myself down the middle with the letter-opener, pull out my contents, read the entrails for signs and hurl myself into the basket.

That's where I am now, along with this article.

And here I intend to stay, unless that damned Willis finds me . . .

CREDO FOR FANTASY WRITERS

(The following oath is recommended to be administered to all professional writers of weird or sf by the editor who purchases their first story. It is suggested that the writer be forced to place his left hand upon a copy of the Necronomicon and raise his right hand in the general direction of the editor's check book, while repeating the following pledge.)

I, John Doe, being of unsound mind and body and otherwise qualified as a potential writer of fantastic fiction, do hereby resolve to adhere to the following restrictions in the practice of my profession, viz, namely and also to wit —

1. Never to write a story about a mad doctor, a mad scientist, or a mad professor.
2. Or even a sane one if that can be avoided.
3. Or, if it can't, never to give one of the above characters a beautiful daughter.
4. Never to write a story about a so-called "giant brain."
5. At least, no more than 6 feet in diameter.
6. Never to write a story about a comical leprechaun.
7. Or a serious leprechaun.
8. Or any lousy leprechaun.
9. Never to write a story about a beautiful native girl named Moola, who turns into a leopard, a black panther, a cobra, a tigress, a vampire bat, a cat or an aardvark.
10. Never to write a story about a timid, weak, poor little clerk who is suddenly gifted with supernatural powers and gets mixed up with a "hardboiled city editor" when he tries to convince him that he can foretell the winner of the Kentucky Derby or the Girls' Intercity Basketball Tournament.

11. I further resolve not to write stories about dinosaur eggs that hatch.
12. Or brontosaurus, pterodactyl, allosaurus, diplodocus, triceratops, stegosaurus or tyrannosaurus eggs that hatch.
13. Or that don't hatch, for that matter.
14. I will not write stories about gallant wipers, oilmen, engineers, pilots, navigators, astrogators or just plain stowaways on spaceships who manage to improvise some last minute solution to keep the spaceship from crashing and then pay for their gallant, heroic effort with their lives as a result of being exposed, during this ordeal, to the deadly fumes or rays of the Sterno which propels the vessel around.
15. I will also try to avoid writing sentences like the above, particularly in the front parts of stories.
16. I will not write stories about Martians who come to Earth and cannot get anyone to believe they are from Mars.
17. I will not write stories about Earthmen who go to Mars and cannot get anyone to believe they are from Earth.
18. I will not write stories about automobiles, airplanes, tractors, or automatic milking machines that come to life.
19. I shall try to avoid tales wherein people are drawn into or out of mirrors, oil paintings, photographs or drawings on privy walls.
20. I will do my best not to write about kingdoms under the sea or kingdoms inside volcanoes or kingdoms inside clouds or kingdoms on the dark side of the Moon, etc. And if I must use such themes I will try to change the kingdoms into republics, democracies or Consumer Coöperatives just in the interest of variety.
21. I shall endeavor to avoid High Priests whenever possible — including the ecclesiastical dignitaries of Atlantis, Mu, Lemuria and all points west. Ditto for priestesses.
22. I leave the problem of "uranium piles" to my physician.
23. I will not write stories about mankind's struggle to rebuild civilization after the destruction of total atomic warfare, nor about mankind's struggle to oust alien conquerors after interplanetary warfare nor about mankind's struggle to repel giant insects, giant reptiles, giant plants, giant robots or giant midgets.
24. While I'm at it I'll avoid all insect, reptile, plant and robot menaces, including the inverted device of making one of the insects, reptiles, plants or robots a friendly character. Anybody who wants to make friends with a giant reptile has my permission to do so — but not for me, thanks — at least not while sober.

25. I shall avoid heroes who will do anything on any planet to anybody for any length of time in order to get enough money to buy drinks.
26. I will not write stories about young men who fall in love with vampires and drive stakes through their hearts to give them "peace."
27. Or about young men who fall in love with ghosts and then commit suicide in order to "join them forever."
28. Or about small boys who can see spirits, werewolves, Elementals, fairies or Martians while their parents scoff.
29. I will eschew the tale of the two lovers who are reincarnated throughout history and get together somehow during World War II in order to die heroically and "live together from now until the end of time."
30. I refuse to write the story about the transplanted brains, hands, eyes or small intestines.
31. Or large intestines.
32. I will not write the story about the civilization where everybody thinks on at least three levels and insists on talking about it.
33. Or not talking about it.
34. It is understood, however, that I will be allowed to disregard any or all of the above restrictions if I get a chance to write one of the above stories for money. After all, a fantasy writer has to eat. Although in view of the above plots one sometimes wonders . . .

IMMODEST PROPOSAL

If we heed the warnings of the prophets, modern man is at present occupying an uneasy seat upon the horns of a dilemma, and is in great danger of (to coin a phrase) a double goosing.

The first horn is labelled *vanishing natural resources*, and its point is that shortly mankind will be faced (or to carry out our figure of speech, reared) with a lack of sufficient raw materials to support present economics throughout the world. The inevitabilitics arc all too apparent.

The second horn is called *increasing population*, and once again we are faced with a seemingly inevitable and inflexible situation, despite the heroic measures promulgated by war-mongers and the international rubber cartels.

There is no need to cite chapter and book to support the dual contention of the scientific prophets who forsee a day when even present marginal living standards throughout the world will crumble in the face of lack of natural resources. Similarly there is little point in questioning vital statistics regarding the birthrate.

We must accept the bitter truth — if the inhabitants of earth continue in their ways, the day of reckoning is at hand, and perhaps even in our lifetime we shall all face the day when universal poverty and starvation is our common lot (even as the late Republican Party predicted).

But defeatism, negativistic thinking, pessimism will get us nowhere. Now is the time for realistic solutions.

Universal rationing of natural resources is not a solution. Such a step is obviously impossible under a free economy or a dictatorship; basic minimum expenditures are unavoidable. And as living standards are raised everywhere, the waste of raw materials can be expected to increase through mathematical progressions. Meanwhile our fields, forests, mountains and valleys are laid bare.

A crisis exists. At this very moment, all over the earth, millions of babies are being weaned. Millions of embryos kick and squirm, and even as these lines are written, millions of impregnations are occurring. By the time this message appears in print, more millions will occur. Let the thinking reader merely attempt to calculate the number of impregnations made in the very short space of time between this article's creation and its appearance and this alone should give him pause.

What is the realistic solution?

We have seen that we cannot halt "progress" whether it appears in the guise of expending natural resources or seminal fluid. The supply of the former seems to be dwindling, whilst the supply of the latter seems inexhaustible and bound to increase because of the increasing birth of boy babies.

We are soon to find a dramatic illustration of our dilemma — an illustration literally brought home to us — when we exhaust our food supply.

The words of the Bible, "Man cannot live by bread alone" will be all too explicit when man discovers that there is no longer any bread.

And yet, perhaps in this very phrase lies the key to our salvation; the realistic solution we have been searching for. The Bible is indeed the repository of all wisdom, and a return to the old-time religion is our only hope.

For ours must be a truly Christian solution. We cannot take inhuman steps; abandon medical progress or modern sanitation methods, in order to increase mortality through plague or famine. We cannot go back to the Dark Ages and keep 90 per cent of the population in serfdom or bondage. There must be equal abundance for all. How will this be achieved in the face of less food and more mouths?

"Man cannot live by bread alone." What solution is implicit in this statement? The unthinking will immediately turn to vitamins and synthetics; unaware that modern science has confessed itself baffled by the problem of actual creation, and that synthetic food as such went out with Henry Wallace.

But the thinking man will anticipate our solution: the only logical, reasonable, practical solution.

Viz.: anthropophagism.

In an effort to consider the physical and psychological problems in modern society, anthropologists and ethnologists have shown an increasing tendency to turn to a study of primitive societies — their manners, mores, customs, folkways. Many valuable contributions to present-day thought have been made as a result of these surveys. Yet for some strange reasons all investigators have chosen to wilfully ignore the implications of the widespread prevalence of cannibalism throughout primitive cultures. Not ritual cannibalism, but *practical* cannibalism. Yet the evidence is there — whenever a savage tribe is faced with a food shortage or famine, cannibalism is the solution and the salvation.

Historians search the past for precedent and precept; they too have ignored cannibalism — if only by dint of superhuman obliquity. For it is not necessary to turn back the clock three thousand years or even three hundred in an effort to find examples. In Germany, during the 1920s, certain butcher-shops had meat. In open boats, during the war years of the 1940s, some castaways waxed sleek and fat.

The pious died. The practical survived. Are we today (all of us in the same open boat) determined to be pious or practical?

We can be both. The followers of the church of Rome, through the daily miracle of transubstantiation, partake of the body of our Lord daily. Would they refuse the offering without transubstantiation? And, logically, if offered a choice between the actual "body of our Lord" and just a plain body, would they not spare the former out of religious fervor and partake of the latter?

Perhaps some will object on the grounds that this is merely Jesuitical thinking — that we are positing a hypothetical necessity.

Yet the problem we face is not hypothetical, but actual; we must deal with actual solutions.

We must find a new way of life in order to survive. And cannibalism is that way of life.

The best way to conserve consumption of natural resources is to consume the consumer.

There is "food for thought!"

In one brilliant stroke, we cut down on the number of mouths to feed and at the same time provide food. We curtail the number of human units that are at present draining us of all natural resources and at the same time provide a *new* natural resource hitherto virtually unexploited.

Let Science come to our aid, as it has come to the aid of Messrs. Armour, Swift and Cudahy. They boast that in their stockyard operations they utilize not only the meat but the by-products. "We use all of the pig but his grunt!" is their boast.

There is no reason for us to do less.

Jonathan Swift's "A Modest Proposal" pointed the way — not only did he suggest that the starving babies of Ireland be made a part of normal *cuisine*, but also that fine gloves could be found in the skins.

This present proposal is, of course, only an outgrowth of Swift's; but we must realize that we are not dealing with satire here but with the realistic approach.

And for the sake of realism, let us for once and for all consider the practical working aspects of cannibalism. Let us devise a suitable *modus operandi.*

Naturally, there are strong tabus to be overcome. We have already considered one; the religious tabu, together with a partial solution based upon theological or physical psychology.

Now let us recognize, boldly, the fact that the majority of us today object to cannibalism upon esthetic grounds. There are ways and means of overcoming these objections; the easiest and most obvious is to employ the semantic approach. We have esthetic blocks which prevent us from enjoying a dish of lamb testicles, intestines, etc — but no objection to dining on lamb-fries, sweetbreads or tripe. Surely the great industrial and advertising minds which have given us "SPAM" and "TREET" can coin suitable neologisms when the time arrives.

But we anticipate. Long before we reach the stage of "packaging a product," we can overcome initial resistance and break down prejudice by proceeding along purely logical paths.

To begin with, we must introduce cannibalism on a small scale, for strictly practical purposes. Instead of penning up habitual criminals for life at great expense to the taxpayer, let us first consider them in terms of calories; of food value. The death-sentence, when rendered, should not be merely a prelude to a useless and expensive funeral. Once this attitude is established, we can then proceed to a consideration of "natural deaths" — and incidentally, point out to the principal objectors, viz, the morticians, that a few simple lessons will transform them into packers and/or chefs without lessening their source of revenue.

Public relations, as we can readily see from this one simple example, will be of inestimable aid in this changeover.

We can next proceed to stamp out both the abortion racket and the stigma of illegitimacy by means too obvious to mention — and as our jails empty so will our orphan asylums. For that matter, our insane asylums will soon be a thing of the past, and perhaps our psychiatrists too in time will turn to cookery and study Brillat-Savarin instead of Krafft-Ebing.

Another oblique approach to breaking down "consumer-resistance" lies in our present program of aid to Europe. The starving are notoriously lacking in fastidiousness; we can substitute ingredients in present CARE packages or our regular shipments abroad. As a matter of fact, we need not even *substitute* — merely by eliminating such shipments entirely we will soon bring about the desired effect and automatically give half the world a tolerance, and gradually a conditioning to cannibalism which will help establish it as a way of life.

After all, it's nothing but setting up a habit pattern. In a world where "dog eat dog" is an accepted business precept; where economic practices are already taken for granted when they cause the deaths of millions, we can hope for still further advances. The course of least resistance will be taken in Europe and in our own America. As meat prices continue to rise, we will find millions turning to some new and ambiguously-labelled packaged meat product which sells for half and contains just as much wholesome nourishment.

By the time criminals, orphans, the insane and handicapped are eliminated, we will find ourselves in the enviable position of having already created a flourishing market and a growing "acceptance" of the new food.

Then subtly, slowly, public relations and business will work with orthodox science to "institutionalize" the practice of cannibalism. Once it becomes fashionable and "smart," the general public will eagerly embrace the practice of anthropophagism. Pictures of society leaders and movie stars "dining out" . . . new "diets" in the women's magazines . . . learned articles in the "business papers" . . . "educational" films . . . radio "jingles" . . . all the resources of modern mass-psychological techniques can be brought to bear upon the problem of promoting popularity for the new food.

Home economists will bear out the fact that this is not a day-dream; potatoes, tomatoes, bananas and other staple articles of diet were once abhorred and regarded with suspicion by the populace — but an educational program won the day.

Our course of life will be changed, naturally. Wars will be fought to take prisoners, not to maim or destroy; this means our civilization will be saved from wholesale destruction and gradually our combative instinct will perish and peace will reign. No longer will there be a "criminal" problem or an "unwanted child" problem or an "insanity" problem. The undesirables will vanish from the earth. Tax-free institutions will go, thus adding to general prosperity. We will find ourselves living in a world of kindly, healthy, tolerant, forward-looking, decent human beings — bright, optimistic, carnivorous.

It won't be done in a day or in a year. But the time is coming and coming fast. Even today in the universal medium, the "comic strip," Mr. Al Capp has unwittingly created a symbol of the shape of things to come — the self-sustaining food product, the "schmoo." As soon as people realize the "schmoo" is merely a symbol of the *human being*, the way to salvation will be clear.

A final word to the timid and finicky — if you have any doubts as to the *taste* of human flesh, be reassured. In the words of those who know through actual experience, human flesh resembles delicious pork or veal. The flesh of tobacco smokers is a bit gamey, but if cigarettes must go, that is in itself a valuable contribution to the health of the race. It is said that when "hung" or aged, flesh has a slightly fishy savor; the comparison is generally made with reference to a salted fish.

To paraphrase the words of the Bible once again, it may not be too long before we are all asking ourselves the ancient question — "Am I my brother's kipper?"

THE BIRTH OF A NOTION

A tragedy of Hollywood
In one act, written and produced by Robert Bloch,
with additional dialogue by Moe Fink, Manny Klotz
and William Shakespeare.

CAST-OFF CHARACTERS:

George Chum — A producer
Ray Sadberry — A Science Fiction Writer
Melvin Spelvin — A Brother-in-Law

The Scene is, if you'll pardon the expression, laid in the Office of the Producer, a lavish two-washroom unit in the San Fernando Valley.

The Time is the present, or a reasonable facsimile of same.

As the curtain rises those of us who are not already asleep discover GEORGE CHUM *seated at his desk, telephoning.*

CHUM: Hello, D.Z.? This is G.C. I just talked to E.B. and he said O.K. I'll get started P.D.Q., see? . . . Well, I'm not quite sure what kind of a picture I'm going to make, no . . . I was planning one of those Biblical things. Biblical . . . that means from the Bible. You know, it's a book . . . whaddya mean, of course I read it . . . well, anyhow, the *Reader's Digest* condensation. Sure. Only the trouble is, there ain't nothing in there that hasn't been made. Except for one part about the Great Whore of Babylon, and that's too hot to handle. Though it'd be a cinch to cast the lead. Huh? Well, I figured if we can't do a Bible yarn we're stuck. No impact, see? What we gonna do for audience appeal if we don't show 'em throwing a lotta Christians to the lions; how we gonna work in torture scenes? You got any other ideas kicking around or do I gotta go back to science fiction again? All right, all right, I'll work it out somehow. After all, it's only a lousy epic.

(CHUM *hangs up and begins to pace the floor, muttering to himself:*)

Now I'm stuck. Another science fiction movie I gotta make yet. Well, that shouldn't be so tough. Actors I got. Technical experts I got. Scenery and costumes I got. Yeah, yeah, so what more do I need? There must be something . . . I'm sure there is . . . now what could it be? Oh — a plot. Suppose I gotta have a plot, too. So . . .

(CHUM *picks up the phone:*)

Hello, get me the Story Department . . . Story Department? This is G.C. I want some information, quick. No, I don't care who won the Fourth at Santa Anita. I already heard. This is business. We're planning another production and I need help. It's science fiction. Whaddya mean you never heard of it? We already made about a dozen. Science fiction — you know, where there's this old scientist guy and his daughter in a black sweater 'n then there's this young scientist who wears glasses in the first scene where he talks about atoms and then takes 'em off when he rescues the girl. Now do you remember? I thought so. Well, we got to have a plot like that, only different. Got anybody down there with some ideas? . . . yeah . . . who? . . . never heard of him . . . oh, send him in, maybe we can work out an angle.

(CHUM *hangs up and sits down. He picks up a copy of* MAD Comics, *then hastily shoves it into a drawer as* RAY SADBERRY *enters.* SADBERRY *is stoop shouldered, bespectacled, an incipient manic-depressive type; in other words, a typical author.*)

SADBERRY: You sent for me, Mr. Chum?
CHUM: That's right. Sit down.
SADBERRY: Er — no thanks. I'd rather stand. You see, I've been sitting in your outer office for the past two months, ever since you hired me.
CHUM: It gets monotonous, doesn't it?

SADBERRY: It gets damned sore, if you want to know. So I'll just stand for a while.

CHUM: Two months, eh? Now I remember — come to think of it, I did hire you, didn't I? Sorry about keeping you waiting, Mr. Badberry.

SADBERRY: Er — Sadberry's the name.

CHUM: My mistake. Now look here, Mr. Gladberry, you're supposed to be an expert on this science fiction crud, isn't that so? Editor, or something?

SADBERRY: (*Stiffly*) A writer, Mr. Chum. I *hate* editors!

CHUM: O.K., you're a writer. Guess that's why I must of hired you, huh? I mean, you're not related to me are you?

SADBERRY: I don't think so. There are no Jukes or Kallikaks in my family tree.

CHUM: Never mind with the Jukes. We ain't making no musical. What I got in mind is one of these science fiction pictures.

SADBERRY: That's what you said when you put me on the payroll. Remember? And I told you this was your great opportunity. Your chance to go down in history as the first man to produce a *real* sf movie. Not one of those phoney yarns about intrepid monsters, but a genuine bit of film art — a prime example of modern sf at its best.

CHUM: Now you're talking. That's just what I'm after — something original, something creative, something that sings. The public is tired of fake Martians and destroying the world. What I want is an entirely new slant; something to make the audience choke on its popcorn.

SADBERRY: (*Solemnly*) Mr. Chum, if that's what you want, I owe you an apology. I'm afraid I've done you a great injustice. Sitting out there all these months, I formed a picture of you as just another typical Hollywood producer, a man who thought only of profits. But if you're interested in the art of the cinema, if you're truly a disciple of science —

CHUM: Believe me, Dadberry, I'm as scientific-minded as they come. Why, I was the first producer in town to install those electric seat-sterilizers in the men's can —

SADBERRY: Well, then, maybe we can work together. Is it a plot you're after?

CHUM: Shadberry, you're a genius! That's exactly what I need for this picture — a plot! You got one?

SADBERRY: As a matter of fact, I have. Do you happen to be familiar with my book *Centigrade 69*?

CHUM: No. I'm not what you call a great reader, Fadberry. Don't have the time. Too busy making pictures to read. Is this yarn any good?

SADBERRY: Well, the critics seemed to like it. It won several prizes and —

CHUM: Never mind with the build-up. What's it all about? What's the title mean, anyhow?

SADBERRY: *Centigrade 69*? Why, that's a temperature reading on a thermometer.

CHUM: (*Jumping up*) Thermometer? Who in hell's gonna make a picture about a thermometer? Where's your sex appeal?

SADBERRY: *Must* it have sex-appeal, Mr. Chum? I mean, you asked for something different.

CHUM: Different, yes. But not queer. You think anybody wants to see a picture about a weather bureau?

SADBERRY: But this isn't about a weather bureau sir. The title refers to the temperature at which —

CHUM: Who cares about the title? That would have to be changed anyhow. *Centigrade 69*, is that a title, I ask you? For science fiction movies, you want a scientific-type title. Something with *Creature* in it, or *Thing* or *Monster*.

SADBERRY: There are no monsters in this story, Mr. Chum.

CHUM: No monsters? Then why are you wasting my time? A science fiction picture without a monster? I never heard of such a thing. Why, it's like an Esther Williams picture without water, a Jane Russell picture where you only see her back! Of all the God-blasted idiots —

(*Enter* MELVIN SPELVIN)

SPELVIN: Duh — youse sent for me, Boss?

CHUM: No. Why should I send for you? I've placed all my bets for the day. Where the devil have you been keeping yourself lately, anyway?

SPELVIN: On the payroll. I been giving dramatic lessons to Alan Ladd.

CHUM: Dramatic lessons?

SPELVIN: You know — acting-like. I got to thinking, see? About all the dough this here Alan Ladd makes on his pitchers, and he alla time only uses one expression, see? So I figgers, suppose maybe he could use *two* expressions — that would be even more sensational. Maybe the pitchers would make twice as much dough. So anyways, I kind of sold the studio on the idea, so I been over on location tryin' to get him to use two expressions. Boy, what a job! Finely I rigged up one of these here electric batteries on a long pole, and when Alan Ladd is in a scene where he sees the heroine, I sort of reach out with this here pole and stick him in the behind and turn on the old juice.

CHUM: (*Interested*) Does it work?

SPELVIN: Well, so far all that's happened is I burned out three batteries.

CHUM: Too bad.

SPELVIN: Well, I ain't given up yet. We're gonna try the same thing with dynamite. (*Notices* SADBERRY.) Who's the character? You castin' for Forest Lawn or somethin'?

CHUM: This is Ray Gadberry. He's a writer.

SPELVIN: (*Ignoring* SADBERRY*'s extended hand*) Well, it takes all kinds, I always say. Pleastameetchasweetheart.

SADBERRY: Are you a writer too?

CHUM: No, this is Melvin Spelvin, my brother-in-law. He's a sort of general all-around — well, just how would you describe your position at the studio, Melvin?

SPELVIN: Why, you just said it. I'm your brother-in-law.

SADBERRY: Is that a full-time occupation?

SPELVIN: Why not? I been on the payroll at a grand a week for the last eight years. You earned a grand a week for eight years, Madberry?

SADBERRY: (*Proudly*) I sir, am a professional author. I am not interested in money!

SPELVIN: And a damned lucky thing it is for you, too, I'll bet. (*Turns to* CHUM.) Well, what else is new?

CHUM: Melvin, we've got a little problem here. Maybe you can help. We're trying to work out a story for a science fiction movie.

SPELVIN: But there *is* a story, isn't there? I mean, you got this old scientist guy and his daughter in a black sweater and —

CHUM: That's just it. We don't want to make that one again.

SPELVIN: I see. The old switcheroo, that's what you're after! Well, suppose you put his daughter in a white sweater for a change.

CHUM: White doesn't photograph well in Technicolor, you know that.

SPELVIN: It could be a thin white sweater.

CHUM: Yes . . . it *could*, at *that*. Maybe you have something there. But it's not enough for a whole picture. We've got to have a plot.

SPELVIN: So that's where Cadberry comes in, ain't it?

SADBERRY: I'm afraid Mr. Chum doesn't see eye to eye with me about plotting, Mr. Spelvin. I did suggest a story.

SPELVIN: Like what, for instance?

SADBERRY: Well, it's called *Centigrade 69*.

SPELVIN: *Centigrade 69*! Stupendous!

CHUM: You *like* it?

SPELVIN: Sure I like it. It's different, it's got novelty, class!

SADBERRY: That's just what I told Mr. Chum. Of course, we gotta change it a little. On account of box-office appeal.

CHUM: Well, what would you suggest?

SPELVIN: Wait a minute . . . lemme turn on my inspiration. (SPELVIN *sits down at the desk, takes a needle from his pocket and gives himself an injection.*)

SADBERRY: (*Whispering to* CHUM) Am I seeing things, or is Mr. Spelvin a narcotics addict?

CHUM: (*Chuckling*) Of course not, Mr. Tadberry. It's only a vitamin shot.

SADBERRY: Oh, I see — hormones!

CHUM: (*Quickly*) Watch your language there!

SPELVIN: Don't be scared, it's just a little shot of *cannabis indica*, like. Want a jolt?

SADBERRY: I don't think so.

SPELVIN: Boy, it really stones me! Now where was I? You were going to change the title, *Centigrade 69.*

SPELVIN: Oh, sure, now I remember. *Centigrade 69, Centigrade 69* — what's cookin' these days? — *Seven Brides For Seven Centigrades* — nah — *Centigrade Life If You Don't Weaken* — *Abbott and Costello Meet Centigrade* — nah — wait — I'm getting it — *Centigrade* means temperature, like, don't it? And temperature means what makes things boil, ain't so? So how about *Centigrade Meets Ma and Pa Kettle*?

SADBERRY: But *Centigrade* isn't a person!

SPELVIN: Of course not. It's a monster.

SADBERRY: No!

SPELVIN: So awright, who needs it anyhow? Knock out the *Centigrade* and what have you got left? A real catchy title. *Ma and Pa Kettle Start Boiling*. How's that?

SADBERRY: But Ma and Pa Kettle have nothing to do with this picture!

SPELVIN: That's just the trouble, ain't it? You said there was no plot. Well, put in Ma and Pa Kettle, and you got your plot ready made!

CHUM: It would cost a fortune to borrow them from Universal.

SPELVIN: So what's a lousy fortune? Think of the angles, sweetheart. Ma and Pa Kettle in a science fiction movie! How's that for a sensation?

SADBERRY: It gives me one, all right. But I don't like to say just where.

SPELVIN: You keep out of this, see? When it comes to plots writers are strickly from hunger. We're gonna do an original, ain't so, sweetheart?

CHUM: *Ma and Pa Kettle Start Boiling*. Hmmm. I can see possibilities here.

SPELVIN: You ain't just woofin', buster! We open with this here Pa Kettle, see? He's fiddlin' around in the woodshed, get me? Been readin' a lotta this here scientific crud like in them Campbell editorials or whatever and he wants he should be a scientist, understand? So right away he's letting his hair grow, he should look like this here Einsteen, or whoever.

CHUM: And Ma Kettle —

SPELVIN: She don't go for it at all, see? Allus takin' after him with the broom-handle and stuff. And one night she sneaks out there and finds out he's been cooking up a whole batch of some kind of chemikles and thinks it's moonshine, got it? And so she dumps it all out on the ground, quick, before the scientist sees it.

SADBERRY: What scientist?

SPELVIN: You know. The young scientist, with glasses. He and some old scientist are with the Revenue Agents looking for moonshine stills. Only the young scientist kind of falls in love with Pa Kettle's daughter.

CHUM: His daughter? How do you picture her?

SPELVIN: Well, I sort of got an idea about a young chick, maybe 18 or so, who went away to the city to college or suchlike and comes back all innarested in this here science herself. She maybe wears one of these here tight sweaters along with her blue jeans.

CHUM: (*Eagerly*) Now things seem to be shaping up!

SPELVIN: Sure. Pa Kettle makes this stuff, Ma Kettle dumps it, and that's where the science fiction comes in. This stuff is alive.

CHUM: Alive?

SPELVIN: Yeah, alive. Pa Kettle, he slipped in enough alky and a whole mess of these here ingredients, like, and he creates some kinda photoplasm —

SADBERRY: You mean protoplasm?

SPELVIN: Photoplasm, like I said. This is a pitcher, ain't it? Anyways this stuff is alive, like and it burns. Everything it touches it burns. That's where the boiling comes in, get it?

CHUM: So the young scientist and the girl try to stop it and —

SPELVIN: Right. And it keeps on rolling and growing, see? We have the scene where it kills this here kid, and we have the scene where the army doesn't believe it, and we have the scene where it starts to roll into Los Angeles and everybody's praying, and the walls start caving in —

CHUM: What about your story-line? What about Ma and Pa Kettle?

SPELVIN: Well, Pa Kettle, he's doing a Paul Revere, unnerstand me? He hitches up this here Francis the Talking Mule and he races ahead of the fire and the Mule keeps yelling, "Fire — run for your lives!"

SADBERRY: (*Groans*) Oh no — we'll have Abbott and Costello in this thing yet!

SPELVIN: You stole my idea! Abbott and Costello, they're friendly Martians, like, up in this here Flying Saucer —

CHUM: What here Flying Saucer?

SPELVIN: The one Ma Kettle contakked on the radio set she built. You see, that's another kicker; she was alla time needlin' Pa for monkeyin' around with science, but she started goofin' through the books and built herself this here ree-ceiver, and it contakked Mars, and so when the fire began to spread she sends out a 505, like, and Abbott and Costello are friendly Martians so they come down in the niche of time and put the fires out.

SADBERRY: How?

SPELVIN: You oughtta know, you write the stuff! Hell, even I know it's real cold up on Mars. So they bring down some super frozen dry ice and blooey! All the fire goes out . . . And Pa Kettle, his britches are on fire, so he just squats down in this here dry ice and wallows around —

CHUM: And the heroine — ?

SPELVIN: They get to her just as her sweater is burnin' off and the scientist hero, he takes the ice and starts rubbin' her —

CHUM: Careful, now!

SPELVIN: So, shoot it and let 'em cut it out in the preview.

CHUM: And the Talking Mule?

SPELVIN: Ma Kettle takes him and goes into business. You see she finds out how good this here special ice is that Abbott and Costello bring down from Mars. So after the fire is out, she has Abbott and Costello bring her a whole lot more, and then she goes out to peddle it in a wagon. And she hitches Francis the Talking Mule up to the wagon, and wherever he pulls it, he hollers out, "Ice for Sale!" to the customers.

SADBERRY: Now I've heard everything!

SPELVIN: Well, thank you. Course, it's still kinda rough, but we can polish it up a little.

CHUM: I'll put a couple writers on it.

SPELVIN: You'll hafta make a deal with Universal — that'll cost. And all that Technicolor . . .

CHUM: Technicolor, *drechicolor!* This is colossal! *Ma and Pa Kettle Start Boiling!*

SADBERRY: Er — wait a minute.

CHUM: Now what?

SADBERRY: Couldn't you manage to keep *Centigrade* in the title somewhere?

CHUM: We just told you, it has no appeal!

SADBERRY: But I've been thinking. Suppose you want to make a sequel? Then you could call it *Son of Centigrade*, or *Centigrade Returns* or *Centigrade Meets the Wolf Man*.

CHUM: Sa-ay! That's not a bad gimmick! Sadberry, there's hope for you yet. Stick around and watch us shoot this picture and maybe you'll pick up our technique here.

SADBERRY: I'll try, sir, I really will. If Mr. Spelvin will help me —

SPELVIN: Sure, glad to give you a couple pointers . . . which reminds me, how about a jolt? (*Brings out needle.*)

SADBERRY: Well — yes. Don't mind if I do! Looks like I'm stuck anyway!

CURTAIN

A LETTER FROM SALLY ANN BLOCH

Hello!

My name is Sally Ann Bloch and I am eleven years old.

My Father got some Magazines from you yesterday and he said to me, Here, take these and read them.

And I said, Why don't you read them yourself, Father Dear?

And he said, I can't, because I'm too Drunk.

And he said, Besides, these are for women. These are Science Fiction Fan Magazines.

So I said, I see. My Father is the greatest Science Fiction Writer in the World. I know, because he told me so.

My Father said, Now read these and then write the editors a letter.

But I don't know anything about Science Fiction, I said.

And a damned good thing too, my Father replied: I will tell you All About It after you are Married.

But, he continued, you don't have to know anything to write letters to these magazines. Besides one of the editors is in the Army in Egypt. And you know something about Egypt, don't you?

Sure, I said. Egypt, with its deserts, its pyramids, its Sphinx.

It certainly does, My Father said. Now be off with you before I get mad and ship you over to Willis.

He is always threatening me like that but he does not mean it. So I Just laughed and took your magazines and read them and they were Very Interesting. Specially like in the first one where you tell about these Conventions.

I know what Conventions are. They are what My Father goes to and then when he comes home he doesn't drink for a whole month, he Just lays there in bed and mutters Oh My God over and over again.

I like reading the letters too. My Father knows some of the people who write you letters. I have not met any of the English ones but I have met Mr. Tucker and Mr. Grennell. Mr. Tucker is like most of the Science Fiction people, but Mr. Grennell is quite Normal. My Father says most of the English people wear beards and those who don't should.

Thank you so much for the Magazines. Well I must go now because there is some kind of trouble. Mother has just hit Father over the head with his bottle again and he is bleeding, and she is calling him a Bloody Provincial.

Hoping you are the same,
Sally Ann Bloch

McGUFFEY'S FIRST SCIENCE FICTION READER

OH SEE THE FUNNY MAN! WHAT IS HIS NAME?

His name, dear children, is Roscoe Krochbinder. He is a writer of sf.

WHY DOES HE WEAR SUCH SHABBY CLOTHES?

Because he is a *fulltime* sf writer. He does not pick up eating-money on the side as a movie projectionist, a television panelist, or a college instructor. He has no other source of income but writing.

CAN'T HE FIND HIMSELF A DECENT JOB?

Well, he tried to become a geek once. But the carnival boss told him he'd have to furnish his own chickens. Besides, he does not want another job. He just wants to write sf for a living.

WHAT IS THE FUNNY MAN DOING?

Right now he has come from a four-hour session of research at the Public Library, where he has been checking material for one of his stories. He is hungry, so he is going into that restaurant to eat.

WHY IS THE WAITER GIVING HIM SUCH A DIRTY LOOK?

Because he only left him a quarter tip. The waiter, a Mr. Fleegle, generally averages about $125 a week in tips.

IS HE A GOOD WAITER?

Well, you'll notice it took fifteen minutes for Roscoe Krochbinder to get waited on. And when he asked for rye toast he got whole-wheat and when he asked for black coffee the waiter brought him coffee with cream in it. You might say he was a pretty average sort of waiter. Nobody complains when a waiter makes a few simple mistakes like that.

WHERE IS MR. KROCHBINDER GOING NOW?

He is taking a bus back to his room to put in another four or five hours of actual writing.

WILL HIS STORY BE FINISHED THEN?

Probably not. He will write a first draft and then he will have to rewrite it.

WHY DOESN'T HE SAVE TIME BY JUST WRITING THE SECOND DRAFT FIRST?

Ha, ha, very funny. Just pay attention to the lesson, please.

LOOK AT MR. KROCHBINDER TALKING TO THE BUS DRIVER. DOES HE KNOW HIM?

Indeed he does. The bus driver, a Mr. Floogle, lives nearby. In a much nicer house, by the way. He drives the same bus on the same route at the same times every day. He likes to talk to people because most of the time he doesn't have much thinking to do on his job.

WHY DID MR. KROCHBINDER BUMP INTO THAT PASSENGER STANDING NEXT TO HIM IN THE BUS?

Because Mr. Krochbinder was thinking very hard. You see, he has to think hard about his stories in order to make sure that he can come up with some new ideas or twists in each one. That's part of his job.

SEE HOW MAD THE OTHER PASSENGER IS!

Well, kiddies, you can hardly blame him. His name is Mr. Fliggle and he has just come from the factory where he is employed as a sweeper. He earns $2.10 an hour for sweeping up — and with his time-and-a-half for overtime and his bonus, he makes about $5,200 a year. He likes the way the union protects him on his job, and he likes his two weeks' vacation with pay, and he likes the idea that the company shells out half of his Social Security and also gives him and his family free insurance. Also, if he gets laid off, he knows he will get Unemployment Compensation. But right now he is mad because he will not get another pay raise until the next round of automatic wage-increases after the steel strike.

THAT IS VERY INTERESTING ABOUT THE AUTOMATIC WAGE-INCREASES. WILL MR. KROCHBINDER GET AN AUTOMATIC INCREASE TOO?

No, dear pupils. Mr. Krochbinder is a freelance writer. He has no fixed salary or income. He has no union or pressure-group to represent him. He gets no pay when he takes a vacation. He must pony up every cent of his Social Security, and make out the long form on his Income Tax return, and do all of his own withholding. Nobody pays for his insurance, and when he retires no company gives him a pension or a bonus. Moreover, there is no such thing as Unemployment Compensation in his life. And as for automatic wage-increases based on a cost-of-living index — hah! Unless he can sell his next story to one of the very few magazines paying top rates, he will send it to one of the other markets. And they will pay him *exactly the same word-rate they were paying writers in 1930, in the depths of the depression!* If, of course, he manages to sell his story at all.

WHAT IS MR. KROCHBINDER DOING NOW?

Sad to say, youngsters, he is walking into the liquor store. Before going home to his room he wants to purchase a pint of rubbing alcohol to put on his sore tonsils.

WHO IS THAT HANDSOME MAN WAITING ON HIM?

That is Mr. Fluggle, the proprietor of the liquor store. He is a neighborhood Big Wheel and clears about $20,000 profit a year.

DOES HE MAKE THE LIQUOR HE SELLS IN HIS STORE?

No, he just buys it from a wholesale house and sells it at retail prices.

DOES HE HAVE TO WORK HARD TO SELL IT?

See how Mr. Krochbinder grabs at that bottle? No, dear students, his customers rush in and take it away from him.

DID HE HAVE TO STUDY TO LEARN HOW TO RUN A LIQUOR STORE?

Certainly not: he never got beyond eighth grade. An accountant handles his books, a stenographer writes his letters, a lawyer handles his business arrangements, the wholesale liquor salesmen provide him with advertising matter and even set up his merchandise for him.

DID MR. KROCHBINDER HAVE TO STUDY TO LEARN HOW TO WRITE?

Oh, a little. After he completed his education, he must have plowed through hundreds of thousands of words before he acquired sufficient skill to sell his stories on a regular basis. He is still learning about writing, and he has to keep up with all sorts of things in order to find material for his yarns.

AND WHAT DID YOU SAY MR. KROCHBINDER EARNS A YEAR?

I didn't say, Nosey. But if you must know, last year his total income — after expenses for supplies and deduction of his agent's commission — was $4,361.

NOT TOO GOOD, WAS IT?

Not too bad, either. Did you know that the over-all *average* income for writers in this country during the same period was only a little over $3,300 for the year, according to an exhaustive survey? And this average includes the earnings of the few big-money men as well as thousands who earned less.

OH WELL, MONEY ISN'T EVERYTHING, IS IT?

That is so right, kiddies. And that is the lesson I want you all to take away from this little exercise. Mr. Krochbinder isn't writing just in hopes of getting rich. He is writing because he actually feels that this sort of work offers him the best outlet for creative satisfaction.

DON'T YOU THINK THESE PEOPLE SORT OF HAVE A SNEAKING ENVY OF MR. KROCHBINDER, EVEN IF THEY MAKE MORE MONEY AT THEIR OWN JOBS?

Well, children, that's a peculiar thing. It so happens that every one of these other men has read some of Mr. Krochbinder's stories at one time or another. I mean, Mr. Fleegle the sloppy waiter — and Mr. Floogle who can drive his bus in his sleep — and Mr. Fliggle who just sweeps up all day — and Mr. Fluggle who holds out a bottle and takes a profit for wrapping it up. They have read Mr. Krochbinder's stories.

DO THEY LIKE MR. KROCHBINDER'S WORK?

More or less. But, you know something? Every one of them has the same complaint. They think Mr. Krochbinder makes too much money.

TOO MUCH MONEY?

That's right. They figure if he only made less, then every story he turned out would be a masterpiece.

BUT IF THESE OTHER PEOPLE DON'T DO SUCH WONDERFUL WORKEVERY DAY ON THEIR JOBS, HOW CAN THEY EXPECT THAT EVERYTHING MR. KROCHBINDER WRITES SHOULD BE EXCEPTIONAL?

Because Mr. Krochbinder is a writer, and writers are supposed to be geniuses.

I DON'T THINK MR. KROCHBINDER IS A GENIUS. I THINK HE IS A DAMNED FOOL.

No comment.

THE TAPE OF THINGS TO COME . . .

As many people who stumbled over his legs can testify, the writer of the following spent a good deal of time at the 1952 Chicago Convention underneath the bed — in fact, more time underneath than is usually spent *in* one. The most charitable opinion presented was that he had merely passed out, but now the truth can be told. He was actually gathering news — as well as lint — for the following article. As a matter of fact, he had a tape-recorder under there with him. Although this may be regarded as a curious choice of companion, he is well satisfied with the results. The following is a transcript of an actual tape-recording, made in the room of a prominent huckster. Naturally, 60% of it — profanity, obscenity and loud cries of "Gimme another drink!" — has been deleted. But the remaining 40% is presented here: unedited, unexpurgated and uncalled-for.

CAMPBELL: Well, folks, I guess you all know what we're here for.
KYLE: Yeah — a fast buck!
ESHBACH: No, not that. (Hastily) Well, not that alone, anyway.
MINES: Sure, we're going to talk about our plans for the next year, aren't we? What we'll publish in the way of magazines, books and anthologies for 1953.
PALMER: Gosh, if the fans knew we got together like this every year and worked things out together, they'd kill us!
BROWNE: You mean they need a reason?
E. GOLD: Let's get organized. I can speak for Horace — he wants to put out some fine —
BOUCHER: I can see you're new here. Never mind that stuff about what

anyone wants to put out. Let's face our problem squarely.

HAMLING: Yes, let's grab the bull by the tail.

KORSHAK: Folks, as I see it we have only one problem. We had it last year and this year it's even worse. We're just plain running out of material.

DIKTY: Sure thing. By Bleiler, in another six months there won't be a single story left to publish! At the rate we're going, with 28 sf and fantasy magazines running —

HAMLING: — and Conklin publishing an anthology a month —

DEL REY: — there just won't be a solitary yarn left to print or reprint! Gentlemen, the situation is serious.

BROWNE: (*apparently waking up*) Serious? Who said anything about a serious? I'm in the market to run a serious of yarns on —

E. GOLD: (*Sweetly*) Shaddup!

B. MAHAFFEY: But we've got to keep going. Can't we just dig up some more authors someplace?

GREENBERG: (*Bitterly*) "Dig up" she says! Take a look at some of the specimens attending this convention and you'll realize that that is just what we have been doing. If the cemetery officials ever find out —

CAMPBELL: This is a grave matter. The condition of the market right now is monstrous!

BROWNE: Monstrous? That's what I want — some stories about Bug-Eyed Monstrous —

PALMER: Please, Howard! Now, as I see it, our problem is this. Every writer we know of is working night and day to grind out stories to fill our magazines, and there still isn't enough material — even tho we're, as usual, trying to write half the stuff ourselves. That's got to stop. It's reached the point where even if I can manage to knock out another story on flying saucers I can't find a writer to do a companion yarn on a flying cup.

KORSHAK: Yes, and to make it worse, I understand that some of the editors who aren't here — Mary Gnaedinger and Dorothy McIlwraith, for instance — are getting so hard up they're even reprinting reprints.

GREENBERG: You think they've got headaches? I happen to know that by June, 1953, there won't be a single story left for any of the forthcoming anthologies. Already, 188 new collections have been scheduled for the year . . . and they don't have 188 yarns.

MINES: Well, here's a suggestion. Suppose we switch things around a bit? I mean, let's get together and throw all our remaining stories into a sort of pool —

KYLE: Yeah, and the deeper the better!

CAMPBELL: Now, let's not be facetious. As a nuclear editor, I must remind you we are facing a serious issue —

HAMLING: We're facing no issue at all, unless we get yarns! Let's hear the rest of Mines' suggestion.

MINES: I was going to say, let's pool all the stories we have on hand and ration them out on a *pro rata* basis —

BROWNE: Basis! That's what I'm looking for! Stories about basis on the moon, basis on Mars, basis on —

ESHBACH: Quiet, or I'll take away your zap-gun. Sam, that sounds like a good idea, but how will that help us hard-cover publishers?

DERLETH: Yes, what about us book publishers? That doesn't find us any new material for anthologies. Up to now, we've had a good thing of it, just reprinting others' reprints, but it can't go on.

BOUCHER: Wait a minute, I think I've got that particular problem solved for you. Has anybody ever complained about this present method of reprinting each other's reprints over and over again in anthologies?

B. MAHAFFEY: No, I guess not, come to think of it. They're actually all the same, really. You know the typical anthology line-up as well as I do.

DEL REY: Sure, "Thunder and Roses," "The Green Hills of Earth," "The Million-Year Picnic," "Knock," "Mimsy Were the Borogoves." Hell, I could edit an anthology with my eyes shut!

E. GOLD: How do you *think* Conklin edits them?

B. MAHAFFEY: Well, the point I'm making is this —

BROWNE: (*Waking*) What's the point? I'll cover that bet —

B. MAHAFFEY: So help me, if I wasn't the Least Bug-Eyed Editor in sf, I'd slug you! Anyhow, what I'm saying is, in anthologies the contents don't matter. As long as you keep on thinking up new titles and new angles for them, the public will keep on buying.

CAMPBELL: Of course! I get it, now. We've had them on "possible worlds" and "invaders" and "time travellers" and a humorous one, and so forth — the gimmick is just to keep putting out the same old stories under new titles, such as —

DIKTY: — *Adventures In Matter and Energy, Impossible Worlds Of Science Fiction, Out Of the Fourth Dimension and Into the Fifth* —

BROWNE: (*Eagerly*) Fifth? Who's got a fifth? Open it up, quick —

HAMLING: (*Ignoring him.*) I get it, now. Just switch the titles, and for sf novels we can do the same thing. Take Doc Smith's books. We can run the same stuff with new names. *The Blue Lensman*, *The Red Lensman*, *The Polka-Dot Lensman* or *Skylark Fourth*, *Skylark Fifth* —

BROWNE: Who's running in the fifth?

PALMER: Sure, who actually reads the stuff anymore?

KORSHAK: (*Excitedly*) Wait. You just said it!

PALMER: Said what?

KORSHAK: You gave us the answer we need. For magazines, too. With 28 going all at once, who *reads* the stuff?

BOUCHER: By McComas, the man's right! Most of the fans have to spend all their waking hours just haunting the newsstands — and believe me, some of the fans here look like they spend their time haunting — in order to pick up the magazines as they come out. There's never enough time for an actual fan to sit down and read!

WILLIAMS: You're right! I was talking to Quinn about that just the other day and we agreed no fan ever reads the stories. No true fan, with a sensitive fannish face, ever buries it in a magazine. He just collects, and trades and mostly he sells the back-issues to other fans —

E. GOLD: Yes, and they collect and trade and sell the back issues to still other fans who —

GREENBERG: Collect, trade and sell to junk-dealers.

BROWNE: (*Heatedly*) Wait a minute, no name calling here, please!

CAMPBELL: Gosh-wow-boy-oh-boy, if that's true, we're saved! Saved, do you hear? All we got to do is keep printing and reprinting the same stuff over and over again. We just change the titles and nobody will ever know the difference.

KORSHAK: But think of the authors. The poor authors! They'll never be able to sell any more new stories!

ESHBACH: Yeah — ha ha — isn't it marvelous?

B. MAHAFFEY: Then it looks like our problem is solved for the coming year. I'm going to double our print order.

HAMLING: I'm going monthly, myself.

WILLIAMS: And I'm printing twice as many titles next year.

MINES: OK, we're all set. We can adjourn until next year. And one final word, hucksters. Remember that oath we all signed in blood — author's blood — that we must keep our little conspiracies a dark secret. No one must ever suspect. Next month I want to see us all writing our usual editorials, taking pot-shots at each other the same as ever. And speaking of pot-shots —

BROWNE: I know. The poker table is all ready. Let's go!

BAH! HUMBUG!

"Robert Bloch sounds to me like an old fan growing sour."

— Randy Brown, *Oopsla* #24

There is probably no more horrifying a phenomenon than the sound of an old fan growing sour. Those who have been so unfortunate as to hear it will never forget the experience. For sheer soul-searing terror, it has country music beat a mile.

Sadly enough, we few old fans who still remain in the thin grey ranks are usually unable to detect our own decadence in terms of decibels. Our senile senses, raddled by long exposure to fannish outcries and deafened by the warwhoops of younger and more vigorous enthusiasts, fail to respond. Besides, we are too close to ourselves; like many an old dog, we can't see the forest for the trees.

I am indebted, therefore, to Randy Brown for thus forcibly calling this matter to my attention, and I cannot hesitate to admit the soft impeachment.

Alas, it is all too true. I *am* an old fan growing sour. Once upon a time I was filled with a sparkling elixir, compounded of two familiar substances; now, one of them has evaporated and all that is left is the vinegar.

But lest Randy be inclined to think too harshly of me for my cranky, morbid, sercon mutterings about fannish affairs, I hasten to raise my feeble voice in a word of explanation.

I know young folks like Randy are naturally impatient with us old gaffers and our continual ill-tempered outbursts and pointless reminiscences, but I'm asking his indulgence here. Forgive an old man his memories, Randy, and I'll try to tell you just what has soured me so dreadfully on fandom, and why I write such nasty, abusive articles as the one which recently aroused your critical perceptivity in *Oopsla.*

Actually, Randy, it's all a matter of disappointment. A man can take just so much frustration in the course of a lifetime and when you reach my age (if you ever do; should you boys down in Texas actually get a World Convention, you'll find it will shorten your life-expectancy considerably) you'll realize that long years of fanning will take their inevitable toll.

Fandom, to me, has been a source of endless disappointment and disillusion. Consider just a few of the disenchantments I've suffered through the years:

They lied to me about my birth. Yes, that's right, Randy; shortly after the time I entered fandom, one of the most prominent fans proclaimed that we lovers of sf were starbegotten. Innocent youth that I was, I proudly rushed in and told this news to my parents. They promptly showed me (a) my birth certificate, and (b) the door. The same fan wanted me to sign up for an organization of super-fen known as the Cosmic Circle, but this proved to be pretty much of a bust. I didn't even get to spend a vacation in the Love Camp in the Ozarks.

They lied to me about ruling the world. All during the late Thirties a group of prominent New York fans were banded together in the belief that sf was a great potential political force. By advancing social and economic doctrines, fans were to assume power in the future. While it is true that a number of these fans have risen to positions of virtual dictatorship (they're magazine editors) I haven't even been able to get a job as dog-catcher.

They lied to me about themselves. During the ages that I've been a fan, I've been the victim of countless deceptions perpetuated by other fans. They told me, for example, that Tucker was dead. Not once, but twice! If this is actually the case, then I sure as hell would like to know who it was that won $1.32 from me at poker in Cincinnati last year. They told me there was a beautiful young femme-fan named Joan Carr, and she turned out to be a rough, tough, brutal Army Sergeant over in England. Still worse, they told me that Boyd Raeburn was a hoax and — cruel and bitter disappointment! — he actually exists.

They lied to me about England. No less a fan than Bea Mahaffey reported to me on how hospitably she had been received during a visit to the London Convention some years ago. She said that all the men had lined up to kiss her. Well, as you know last year a whole plane-full of American fans went over there for a Convention. I checked recently with Bob Silverberg, who attended the Con, and he swears up and down that those hospitality reports are a lie — not a single man even offered to kiss him.

They lie about everything. As a faithful reader of sf, I read everything Richard Shaver wrote and not once was I able to remember Lemuria, nor have I so much as seen a single Dero (except, of course, at conventions). I studied Dianetics, but I never became a one-shot clear — in fact, I can still drink as many as ten shots and all that happens is I get foggier than ever. I bought a Heironymous Machine but it isn't even sticky enough to seal envelopes with.

No, an elderly fan like myself can endure only so much without cracking. After all, I'm a mere mortal, not a Texan. And thus it is, when confronted with the fakery and falsity of fandom I totter to my feet, brandish my truss, and croak:

"Fandom? Bah! Humbug!"

I'LL FRY TOMORROW

I had come to the end of my rope.

Sitting alone in that shabby little room on Skid Row I stared at my haggard, bloated face in the mirror.

Was this really me? If so, what had become of the charming youngster who had laughed and sung and danced her way through life? What had become of the golden friends of the golden years? I sighed and reached for the bottle with trembling hands. Carefully I tilted it forward, then sprang up with a curse.

The bottle was empty.

The *last* bottle was empty!

I held it upside down, shaking it in despair, but I knew the truth then.

There wasn't a drop of mimeograph ink left. Now I would never get my fanzine out. I, Ellen Harlison, was finished. There would never be another issue of *Pretensions*. The room reeled before my eyes and I fell back upon a pile of correspondence.

Aimlessly I opened 15 or 20 of today's fan letters, but I found myself too nervous even to read the enclosed quote cards. I reached for a prozine, spat upon its cover, then dragged myself to the typer to compose a letter of helpful critical advice to the editor.

Dear Sir, I typed, *Your last issue stinks*. Then I found I could not go on. I could no longer escape the truth. My eyes inevitably strayed to the corner where I had piled the unfinished portion of *Pretensions* already run off. A mere 1,000 copies each of the first 234 pages. I, who had boasted an edition of 10,000; of a full 500-page fanzine with justified edges and unjustified interlineations! The mere sight of those looming piles was too much. Trembling, I picked up the phone and dialed a number before my courage failed me.

"Hello," I quavered, "This is Ellen Harlison. I need help, quick!"

The voice on the other end of the wire was calm, cheerful. "Fanzine trouble?" it inquired.

"Yes. It's my piles. I look at them and I can't sit still. Oh, the itching, burning torture — "

"Be right over . . ."

The voice clicked off and I staggered across the room, frantic with the realization that I had completely lost my grip. My grip, already packed for the next convention, and containing everything I had planned to huckster off in the lobby — the placards reading YNGVI IS A GOOD MAN, and DEAN A. GRENNELL IS A LOUSE, the Eney for TAFF buttons, the original Ivar Jorgenson manuscript and all the rest.

It was gone. Everything was gone. Voices mocked me from the corners of the darkened room.

"You sawed Courtney's boat! Fake-faaaan! You have no sense of wonder. Why don't you go on into FAPA and die?"

"No!" I screamed.

But the voices continued: dreadful booming voices that sounded like Moskowitz with his head in a barrel or a bunch of Canadians holding a party in their room. I ought to know, because I could remember when I was the party being held.

"Go away!" I shouted, tossing a handful of half-completed stencils at the mirror. The tracings of the Rotsler drawings fell to the floor and I stepped on them. I'd always heard about how some men have the ambition to walk on acres of those things, but it didn't give me a thrill. I just got blue ink all over my feet. My feet were cold. Suddenly I sneezed. "Achoo!"

"Gestetner!" said a polite voice behind me. I wheeled and confronted the intruder.

"Who are you?" I whimpered.

"You called a while ago?" The stranger was calm. "I'm from the organization."

"Yes," I faltered. "I remember now. But it's no use. I don't think you can help me. It's too late."

"Sit down, my child," said the stranger, taking my hand in his. His fatherly manner reminded me of Tucker. "It's never too late. Just tell me how it happened."

Before I knew it, I was pouring out my heart to this quiet, understanding man.

I told him how it had all begun, years ago, when my friends lured me into a magazine store and urged me to buy my first copy of *MAD Comics*. How, slowly but imperceptibly, I worked my way up to *POGO* — reading, at first, only in spare moments or public washrooms. Then came my introduction to sf, a logical step forward. Before I realized it I was off on a *Galaxy* kick, then switched to *Astounding*. Within a year I was reading two magazines a week — sometimes mixing *MoF&SF* with *Amazing* just to give me an extra thrill. From there there was no turning back. Somewhere along the line, unbeknownst even to myself, I crossed over into fandom. Starting with the "harmless" *MAD Comics*, I had graduated imperceptibly to *Hyphen*, *Grue*, *Oopsla!*, *A Bas* and even worse. Inevitably I began to "correspond" with other addicts — people like Chuck Harris, Charles Harris, Vernon McCain; rabid fans like Redd Boggs and his partner, the notorious Henry Thoreau.

"I thought I had it under control," I confessed. "But the fanzines started rolling in and I found myself reading two and three a day, cover to cover, without stopping. I began to mail out quote cards and enter into hoaxes. I went to conventions and bid at the auctions. It got so I didn't care about my reputation any more — I once had a hotel room on the same floor as damon knight.

"Pretty soon I was trying to get into FAPA. I knew it was certain death, but I didn't care. I put out the first issue of *Pretensions* — a mere 200 pages — and started to assemble the second 500 page issue. Then something happened to me. I found that I was falling farther and farther behind. Now the mailing is ready and to my horror I realize I've been delaying for two months. What's a girl to do?"

The stranger patted my hand consolingly. "You can give it up if you really want to," he said.

"I can't. I've gone too far. You know what I am," I whispered?

"Of course," he sighed. "But let me tell you a little story."

He cleared his throat and continued.

"You may not believe it, my dear, but I was once a fugghead just like you. Perhaps even worse than you, because I was a serious constructive fugghead. I contributed to the TAFF and even attended the Business Meetings at conventions. I joined a fan club in my home town and one year we even put in a convention bid — though Ghod was good to us and we lost by 20 votes and two fifths of Jack Daniels.

"I thought I could take it or leave it alone, but you know what happened. I began to neglect my work, my friends, my very drinking, in favor of fanning. Then one day I found myself at a Midwescon, playing poker with Tucker. Suddenly a wave of realization swept over me. 'What am I doing here ?' I asked myself. 'How low can a man sink?' Throwing down my cards — and scooping up the pot — I rushed out into the night and wandered down a lonely Ohio road.

"A car pulled up alongside me and a kindly voice bid me enter. I did so and found myself in the hands of the State Police. It seems Tucker had issued a complaint, claiming I had stolen his ten of clubs from the game. (The one with the earmuffs.)

"My trial was a hollow mockery, but I was so deeply immersed in misery that I paid no heed. I accepted my sentence of a year in the penitentiary without a murmur. Soon I was occupying a cell. And it was there that I found my salvation.

"My cellmate was a kindly old rapist from the East. Discussion of his exploits inevitably reminded me of conventions. I began to talk about them, and to my surprise found that he himself was a former BNF. In fact, he had once been a member of the Hydra Club —

"And yet this man — whose name I'm sure you'd recognize — was to all intents and purposes completely cured. He did not receive a single letter from a fan during all the time I spent with him, nor did he send out as much as a scurrilous poctsarcd to Willis. He never read a fanzine or prozine, although many of those containing Nancy Share illustrations were being smuggled throughout the prison.

"What impressed me even more, he was capable of discussing fandom without the slightest hesitation. I'll never forget one remark he made to me after I'd been in prison about six months.

" 'Fandom,' he said, 'is just a goddamn hobby.'

"I began to think about that. And when I came to realize the truth of this statement, the turning-point arrived. I asked my cellmate for the secret of how to free myself from the habit. And it was he who put me in touch with Fuggheads Anonymous.

"Upon my release from prison I immediately sought out the local chapter of the organization. I worked with them for another year. Oh, it wasn't easy, I assure you, and there were many times when I was tempted to backslide into the mire. But I found my solution in helping others, such as yourself."

I nodded. "Do you think you can help me?"

He smiled. "I can try. The first thing to do is get rid of this mess." He pointed to the stack of paper standing next to my mimeograph.

We set to work with a will.

From then on, mine is a history of painful but persistent progress. Once I got rid of my piles, I was able to sell the mimeograph. The whiskey bought with the proceeds enabled me to win the friendship and the confidence of the local Fuggheads Anonymous chapter in my community.

I learned that I was not alone in my terrifying battle against the ravages of acute fandomania. A man from California, who had once been a member of the notorious LASFS. A Minnesota resident, and a Florida fan who had actually met Walter A. Willis. A former Missourian, now in the Navy; even a girl about my age who stablized herself by buying a horse.

Our weekly meetings are held in a little hall downtown, and every member is required to attend. Generally we devote a certain amount of time to discussing each other's past fuggheadedness, and give testimony of our thanks at escaping from the clutches of organized fandom.

Sometimes we have a little program with speakers, and we often invite fuggheads from other parts of the country to be our guests. You see, we have a great number of correspondents here and abroad, and many of us now print up little Fuggheads Anonymous magazines for general distribution. Our membership is limited to seventy-five at the present time, but we have about forty-two on our waiting list. Perhaps next year we'll hold a sort of get-together or convention.

So you see, I have found it easy to forget fandom. Fuggheads Anonymous has given me a new outlook. And I'm writing to that rapist in prison too. When he gets out he has promised to start a new life with me.

But one of these days you can read it all. I intend to write it up in my own magazine — a little 750-page effort which I call *Dissentions*. Goshwowoboyoboy, wait until you see this issue! You'll blow the propeller right off your beanie —

"FORTY WHACKS"

It is somewhat hard for me to realize that, as of April 5th, 1957, I shall be forty years old.

As a matter of fact, I have no intention of admitting it. When people ask me point-blank, I generally fob them off with some ambiguous remark — such as saying, "Yes, I am a member of the Fortean Society."

But the cold truth confronts me, and I can only confront it in turn.

Forty.

Up until recently, it seemed an incredible age for anyone to attain. Being forty years old was something which only happened to other people, like Forry Ackerman, or which *might* happen to others, such as Jack Benny. In the latter case, I wouldn't feel much pity, since Benny is at least compensated by his wealth. In the former case, of course, I'd feel no pity at all, because Ackerman is an agent and *nobody* wastes pity on an agent.

Actually the forty problem didn't really bother me until a few weeks ago, as the fatal hour drew near.

Then suddenly, everywhere I went, references began popping up. Picked up a paper and there was a mention of Pitkin's *Life Begins At Forty*. Opened a book, and out popped the Lizzie Borden quatrain about "forty whacks." After burning the newspaper *and* the book, I hastily turned on the TV set to encounter a cartoon about *Ali Baba and the Forty Thieves*. Smashing the picture-tube, I sought consolation in the Bible. What happens? The first line I encountered reads, "And rain fell upon the earth forty days and forty nights."

In despair, I fled to Chicago to deliver a lecture and a less formal talk. The latter was presented to the University of Chicago Science Fiction Club. It's a bright, youthful organization and I've always enjoyed myself when visiting with its members. But when I rose to speak I was introduced by Sidney Coleman, who immediately remarked to the audience that, "Bloch had his first story published before I was born."

Now I don't know what he meant to convey by that remark; maybe the idea of coupling two calamities in one sentence seemed appropriate to him.

But for me, that tore it.

Ever since I've been brooding over the future, and so far I can discern only a single ray of hope.

Other fans will turn forty, too, in the decade to come.

Misery loves company, and believe me, the WELCOME mat is out.

I can't wait until we're all in the same boat and bailing like crazy. At first I was going to give up fandom — or at least the most important aspects of fanning (viz: hot-rods, rock-and-roll, progressive jazz and boycotting *Infinity*). I was even seriously thinking of giving up conventions: after all, a man can make a damned fool of himself at home, too.

Then I began to realize that before too many years have passed, the majority of convention-goers are going to find themselves in the same age-bracket.

Against that day, I respectfully submit a program for the 1967 *World Science Fiction Convention and G.A.R. Reunion,* to be held at the Old People's Home in the suburbs of Fort Mudge.

OPENING SESSION: 1 P.M.

Introductory remarks . . . . Sam Moskowitz

(*Ear-trumpets will be provided to the audience for those who wish to hear Mr. Moskowitz plainly.*)

Address: "Science and Senility" . . . . Wilson Tucker Auction

(*Souvenir canes, wheel chairs and other valuable items of interest to present-day fandom will be offered at attractive prices.*)

EVENING SESSION: 6 P.M.

Banquet

(*Milk-toast optional: however no solid food will be served unless fan provides his own teeth or rents a set from the convention committee.*)

Main Address: "Why I gave up Psionics and turned to Geriatrics" . . . . John W. Campbell, Jr.

I could go on for a three-day session, but I'm quite sure that the attendees can't. As a matter of fact, the evening session will probably close by 8 P.M. at the latest. The lights will go out by nine — not that it matters, because nobody will have the strength to take advantage of it. I doubt if there will be any "incidents" at all. I can hardly see anyone trying to break down the door to Harlan Ellison's iron lung.

In a way, come to reflect upon it, this new era in future fandom may be a good thing. Like it or not, fans will attain the respectability and dignity of maturity. No more of this business of tossing bags of hot water out of windows: most of us will think twice about dropping out hot water bottles, even if we can still open a window. We'll have a little peace and quiet for a change; leave the rioting to kids like Doc Smith.

As for me, I'm content to join all the loveable old codgers at the Hydra Club — folks like Uncle Bob Silverberg and sf's beloved Elder Statesman, Randy Garrett.

Maybe I'm a little bit too self-conscious about the passage of time, but I can't help thinking that our microcosm is coming of age. The helicopter beanie, once a standby of active, youthful fandom, is due to be replaced by a more appropriate symbol.

May I suggest a jet-propelled truss?

THROUGH A PICTURE-TUBE, DARKLY

I became a writer of television scripts back in 1950, and began making more or less regular appearances as a television performer in 1953. But it was not until the last month of 1956 that I became a member of the television audience. As a script-writer, I had learned a few things about children's show material, how to do hard-sell and soft-sell commercials and the best method for pleasing any sponsor (viz.: eliminate the show entirely and run a continuous advertisement). As a performer, I exchanged witticisms with an unending succession of night-club comics, second-string stage and screen celebrities, baseball players, musicians, orchestra conductors and young ladies who owed their appearance on a quiz show more to their mammaries than to their memories.

But it took the last fourteen months as a television viewer to really complete my education. During this period I have learned more about life in this great world of ours (mostly yours; in fact it's *all* yours, because *I* want no part of it) than ever before. Truly, television is an enlightening force. The old truism that travel broadens one applies doubly to television. It is impossible to remain seated before a TV screen for fourteen months without broadening considerably.

Here then, are a few of the things about life which I never realized until I discovered them, thanks to the electronic miracle of television:

1). All boys, up to the age of 18, are nice. They address every adult male as "sir," and when greatly provoked, they say, "Gosh!" or "Gee!" They live in expensively-furnished white suburban homes, with parents who never quarrel, due to their wonderful sense of humor. When they go out on dates, they wear tuxedoes and bring a corsage for their girls. If the boys are preadolescent, they usually have some sort of very intelligent pet and a loveable Grandpop. This presents no problem, because the entire family is crazy about animals. Television boys do not smoke, drink, swear or draw pictures on lavatory walls; there isn't an artist in the entire crowd in fact.

2). Television boys between the ages of 18 and 26 become "juvenile delinquents." They wear leather jackets and their curly hair is uncombed. They don't live in homes, although sometimes, when wanted for murder, they invade the homes of exurbanites for a brief stay until the head of the house outwits them. They are usually mentally disturbed and often speak with a southern accent. Sometimes, of course, they are members of a city gang, in which case they terrorize innocent girls.

3). Families in the $20,000-$30,000 a year bracket have serious problems. More accurately, they have *a* serious problem: how will the husband manage to become vice-president of the company? It is possible (nay, inevitable) that the best part of an hour will be spent in attempts to wangle such a promotion from the boss. Exactly four minutes before the final commercial, the husband will transform apparent failure into brilliant success and win the coveted position. During the next three minutes he will search his soul, wondering if he really and truly wants material success after all. During the last minute he and his wife will become reconciled to accepting the job, much to the surprise of every three-year-old child in the audience.

4). Many people (particularly comely young women and handsome young men) are subject to "temporary amnesia," during which time they suspect themselves of having committed a murder. Actually, of course, they are innocent; the murder was really committed by some older and uglier person. This is a matter which can be cleared up by any competent psychiatrist.

5). Competent psychiatrists are able to straighten out virtually all personality-disorders in one two-minute monologue. Anyone suffering from a mental disturbance is automatically "cured" when a psychiatrist reveals its source. In non-technical terminology, that is. Stuff like "cathexis" sounds too dirty for the audience.

6). There is no such thing as a married cowboy.

7). No "private eye" has ever failed to solve a case.

8). It is impossible to produce an hour long "variety show" without including, somewhere along the line, a surrealistic set as the background for a dance-routine. This routine is performed by a girl who may or may not sing in addition. But no matter the nature of the set itself or the talents of the girl, she is always surrounded by four posturing males in black, skin-tight pants. Up until July, 1957, this number called for *six* males. Since then, apparently, the union minimum for dancers has been lowered, so now it's just four. The *same* four, I suspect, on every show. My suspicions are also directed toward the masculinity of the dancers.

9). On the aforesaid "variety show" of which I speak, it is impossible to address any performer by his or her last name.

10). All guest-stars have just released a "new album" (*Music to Shave Your Legs By*) which must be held up and plugged by the M.C. before the performer is introduced. In return, the guest star will mention that the M.C. has also just released a new album (*Music To Listen To While Waiting For a Laxative To Take Effect*) and if the show is a particularly pretentious one, there will be a final announcement to the effect that the whole programme has been recorded, and will be released in a new album, *Music To Take the Place Of A Laxative.*

11). Really *big* television shows are called "spectaculars," which is a technical term meaning "dramatized fairy-tales."

12). The human body is a marvelous mechanism, consisting of the "mouth," a small opening, and a short tube extending into a large space known as a "stomach." This entire area serves as a racetrack for a bunch of pills.

13). Cartoon animals spend most of their time jumping up and down and singing the praises of various brands of toilet paper.

14). It is impossible to smoke a modern cigarette unless you are an experienced outdoorsman and a trained athlete.

15). Every automobile is the lowest of the low-priced three, only it costs more.

16). Most television sets themselves are marvelous and complicated instruments, and sometimes it takes half an hour to find the little switch that will turn the TV off.

17). It's usually worth the effort to do so.

IN MEMORIAM: W.T.

Once upon a time, boys and girls, there was no *MAD Comics*. Once upon a time there was no *POGO*. Yes . . . and believe it or not . . . there wasn't even a Stan Kenton! In those primitive days, before the coming of trimmed edges and digest-sized magazines, sf fans were few and far between . . . no one had ever conceived of a convention, the first fanzine had yet to be published, and the beanie hadn't even been invented.

What do you suppose fans did in the Dawn Ages? You'll probably never guess, so I'll tell you. They read magazines!

And one of the magazines they read was *Weird Tales*. They read it thirty years ago . . . before there was such a publication as *Amazing*; before *Wonder* and *Astounding* came into existence . . . when there wasn't even the faintest cloud looming on the horizon as a prelude to *The Immortal Storm*.

Since then a full generation has passed. Thirty years have come and gone. And *Weird Tales* is no more.

I am woad-painted and keening over its demise, but a bit regretful that I don't detect more mourners at the funeral. As I write these lines, however, I've yet to see any mention of *Weird Tales*' passing in the current fanzines. Not so much as an interlineation disturbs the endless references to *MAD*, *POGO*, cool jazz, Courtney and other topics of interest to the Serious Constructive Fan of Today. I dare say that many of the more eminent authorities on Brubeck and Little Willie have never heard of *Weird Tales*. I am quite certain that an even greater number may have noted patronizing or disparaging references to the publication but didn't read it.

Indeed, for the past ten years or so it was quite the fashion to dismiss *Weird Tales* as a fantasy magazine of interest only to the oldtime followers of H. P.

Lovecraft — as such it wasn't worth the attention of readers who paid allegiance to contemporary authors in the science-fantasy genre.

But now that *Weird Tales* has gone to the Happy Haunting-Ground, it may be permissible to remind some of the late-comers that a giant has fallen.

For during the first 20 years of its existence, it played a highly important part in the development of the science-fantasy field. Under Edwin Baird, Farnsworth Wright and the early editorship of Dorothy McIlwraith, *Weird Tales* made signal contributions.

A surprisingly high percentage of today's "big names" did their early work in *Weird Tales'* pages.

It may come as a shock to contemporary fans to scan a list of *Weird Tales* contributors and note such names as Heinlein, van Vogt, Boucher, de Camp, Pratt, Sturgeon, Williamson, Simak and others of similar stature.

Many do not realize that *Weird Tales* printed the first professional work of Henry Kuttner, C.L. Moore, Fritz Leiber, August Derleth — that *Weird Tales* developed the talents of many "old-timers" in the field such as Long, Wandrei, Binder, Edmond Hamilton — that for years Ray Bradbury spent his time trying to crack *Weird Tales* rather than *The Saturday Evening Post* — and that *Weird Tales* was making the honorable mentions list of the O'Brien and O. Henry yearbooks as far back as 25 years ago.

Weird Tales developed artists like Bok and Finlay . . . served as the creative cradle for "classic" characters such as Conan, Jirel and Northwest Smith . . . printed the early del Rey and Cartmill and set the pattern for the later *Unknown*. Fredric Brown, Manly Wade Wellman, Eric Frank Russell, Nelson Bond — the list of *Weird Tales'* contributors is an *Almanac de Gotha* of Gothic stylists who later came to concentrate on the more lucrative straight sf markets.

And yet, to many a writer in the "great years" of *Weird Tales'* history, the publication of a story in its pages — even at lesser rates — was a desirable achievement. I well remember Stanley Weinbaum telling me, only a few months before his death, that he wanted desperately to write a yarn that would "hit" *Weird Tales*, for at that time (incredible as it may seem to those who are familiar only with recent developments) publication in *Weird Tales* carried with it a prestige value; insofar as it was the only magazine of its kind to enjoy critical recognition. *Weird Tales* stories were reprinted generally in anthologies long before the war brought the "sf boom" into being. For many authors, writing for *Weird Tales* was a labor of love.

It was always thus with its "great years" editor, Farnsworth Wright. Wright remains one of the forgotten heroes today; but hero he was, in every sense of the word. The ravages of Parkinson's disease failed to quell a brilliant intellect, holarly and critically keen editorial insight, an inordinately keen sense of ıor and above all, a genuine devotion to fantasy literature which had no tion to the profit-motive. *Weird Tales* never made money for anyone — lishers, editors, writers or artists — but it made friends. It made progress the field. As a developing-ground for talent, *Weird Tales* contributed as :h or more than any other single magazine. Though its accent on fantasy horror may seem dated and distasteful today, it is impossible to dismiss illustrious roster of talent which found first fruition within its pages. *Weird :s* needs no *apologia* . . . or for that matter, epitaph. The magazine may be d, but its influence lives on, and will continue to flourish for many years to ıe. *Sic Transit, gorier!*

LOST AND FOUND DEPARTMENT

I was particularly stricken with Al Toth's enlightening report on the contents of a 1938 *Astounding* in *Hodge-Podge* #9. So much so that I rushed over to the book shelves and dug out a yellowing copy of the January, 1935 *Weird Tales*. Al Toth wanted to know what the ads were like in 1926 . . . sorry I can't oblige him, because (contrary to vile rumors) I wasn't doing any pro writing in '26. But here, for what it's worth, is the 1935 *Weird Tales* ad lineup.

STOP DANDRUFF AND FALLING HAIR says the first headline. Unfortunately, somebody has bitten a big piece out of the page just below this admonition and I can't imagine what the rest of the ad said. I'd assume, from the caption, that they were selling some kind of hairnet designed to catch dandruff and hair when it fell . . .

HYPNOTIZE . . . GAIN LOVE, FAME AND FORTUNE, CONTROL OTHERS. Complete course of instruction. Oriental Secrets, 26 lessons. Become a master of colossal power. Limited time only, $1.50. Dr. Charlemagne, out in Seattle, Washington, offered this bargain. And believe me, it *is* a bargain, girls. All those Oriental Secrets (funny, I never thought of Seattle as being in the Orient before) plus becoming a Master of Colossal Power — and for only a buck and a half, yet! Just goes to show how far your money would go in the depression. Why today you couldn't *touch* a course that would give you Love, Fame, Fortune and the Control of Others for less than $4.75. And I'll bet they wouldn't even throw in any of those Oriental Secrets, either!

Next we come to LONESOME? LET ME ARRANGE A ROMANTIC CORRESPONDENCE FOR YOU. And so on. Evan Moore, of Jacksonville, Florida is the guy to write to, apparently. Interested?

How about VICTORY OVER AGEING? Not by drugs: With a Cream

Embrocation acting instantly, better than all tonics. Results guaranteed. The tube only $1.00 from Luc Prouvosky, M.D.

There you are, kids. A buck and a half to Doc Charlemagne for love, fame and fortune and the secrets of the orient. Another buck for youth. $2.50 gives you a complete deal. Ah, that good old depression! If only I'd had $2.50 then!

Now we come to CURIOUS BOOKS PRIVATELY PRINTED. Oriental love, Uncensored Exotics, Amatory Adventures and other Curious Sex Customs. That's the come-on offered for the free catalog of the Panurge Press, but it might make a good ad for a fanzine today, huh?

On the next page you can become a DISTRICT MANAGER (flavors, spices, cosmetics) or take 62 ART LESSONS BECOME TALENTED ARTIST WITH BIG INCOME, NATURAL ABILITY NOT NECESSARY. As if we didn't know it after looking at some of the illos in the 'zines. That cost $1.95 or 45¢ more than love, fame and fortune. Even in those days, people *valued* art over mundane things, apparently.

And now we come to a favorite of old and young alike . . . one of the Immortal Classics of Advertising . . . reproduced word for word, thousands upon thousands of times, and still as punchy, as vital, as compelling as the first day its inspirational message challenged readers in the dawn of Time. Yes friends, it's PILES — DON'T BE CUT UNTIL YOU TRY THIS WONDERFUL TREATMENT. And the sample is *free!*

Ah, that depression! For only 10¢ you are next invited to sample a copy of AMERICA'S LARGEST, MOST ROMANTIC AND TRULY PULSE QUICKENING SOCIAL MAGAZINE filled brim full with human interest personal descriptions and photos of truly lovable ladies and worthy gentlemen seeking sincere pen-pals and lasting happiness . . . CUPID'S INTERNATIONAL MESSENGER. *This* one is really good. I *know*, because back in 1935 I sent my dime and I met Bob Tucker that way.

Now, here's a snappy opportunity for all *Weird Tales* readers. MAKE MONEY AT HOME. GROW MUSHROOMS IN YOUR CELLAR! Enormous new demand . . . free book. Think of the thousands upon thousands of creeps who read *Weird Tales* back in '35 . . . people like little Henry Kuttner and young Miss Moore and baby Ray Bradbury who took advantage of this chance to start on the road to financial independence by growing mushrooms in the dank catacombs of their typical *Weird Tales* reader type homes! It is enough to give one pause. Plus fur and a tail.

Oops! MEMBERS OF THE FUTURIST SOCIETY ARE MANY YEARS AHEAD OF THEIR TIME . . . They know more, earn more, live more fully than most other groups of people . . . join . . . instead of a slave, you become a ruler of this planet! Hmm. D'ja suppose that's the way Arthur Godfrey got — naaa, it *couldn't* be! *Could* it?

HOROSCOPE and BE A DETECTIVE and SELL BY MAIL and WE PURCHASE ALL INDIAN HEAD PENNIES and FILMS DEVELOPED and a dozen more LONELY? ads, several featuring Wealthy Members. You still see 'em today. But what about HAPPINESS INSURED? Here you get . . . rare and intimate knowledge of life forces daringly revealed in a SPECIAL BOOK. It was formerly $1.00, now 50¢ postpaid. Sounds like a good deal especially when you consider that 50¢ price. Because, on the same page, for a buck, double the money, all you get is RARE BOOKS, CARTOONS, PHOTOGRAPHY, 20 SNAPPY SAMPLES. Might be pretty hot stuff but there's no Happiness Insurance along with it.

Next we come to BAR BELLS ARE THE GREATEST BODY DEVELOPERS . . . if you want to get enormous development.

And out in California Ben Hobbs (J. Ben Hobbs) offers LET MY SPIRITUAL INSIGHT HELP YOU . . . I am an understanding friend with whom you can discuss your most secret personal affairs in strictest confidence. Advice, $1.00. (My advice, belated as it is, would be not to trust this joker. That'll be one dollar, please.)

Down in Chambersburg, Pennsylvania you can buy MYSTIC CURIOS, PSYCHIC AIDS, RARE NOVELTIES. What's a "psychic aid," I wonder? Sounds like a truss ad for ghosts.

And from El Paso comes glad tidings of DIVORCES IN MEXICO . . . probably for the benefit of those who haven't made the right wealthy connection in one of the Lonesome Clubs.

Right here in Wisconsin, up at Adell, you could buy WEIRD LIQUID LIGHT pocket lamp Formula: only a dime. Though who in hell wants to carry a liquid light around in his pocket?

On the back page, FIRESTONE AND GOODRICH TIRES, reconditioned, low as $2.15. Cheap enough, but remember, you could buy a used car for $10. With 5 tires!

Oh that depression! Oh, to be depressed again — what joy! Next time we go into an economic collapse, I'm gonna look me up one of those Secret Mastery of the Universe deals for a buck or so, go around hypnotizing everybody in sight, marry rich, become a private detective and fill the whole damned basement with the biggest mushrooms you ever saw. And say, if you want any Snappy Cartoon Books, you just come around and ask!

THE DEMOLISHED FAN

I happened to be going through my files the other day and when I got as far as "F" (for Fingernails) I came across a small section labelled FANS. This so intrigued me that I crawled right out of my files again, banging my head on the drawer, and sat down to contemplate the *memorabilia* of another day. (Memorabilia, for the benefit of those who came in on free passes, is a fancy name for the kind of thing you look at and say, "I wonder what the hell I saved this old crud for?")

But there it was . . . a dusty, musty bundle of fanzines containing my own minute contributions to the field. Now unlike the Big Names — men like Wilson Tucker and Dr. David H. Keller, M.D. — I have never made a regular habit of writing for amateur publications. In recent years I've been a bit more active in this direction, having published a number of items under the pseudonyms of Walter Willis, Lee Hoffman, Harlan Ellison and Hugo Gernsback — but no great volume. Still, I was surprised at the number of magazines represented.

And it occurred to me that, in a piddling sort of way, I had amassed through the years a sort of capsule History of Fandom. The kind of capsule you take with a glass of water and a fervent prayer that this will put you to sleep, that is. So while you're sleeping, I'm going to take a casual ramble through Memory Lane, and let the toes stub where they may.

The first item I picked up is a little orange-covered magazine titled *Marvel Tales*. It's a printed job from Everett, Pennsylvania, dated 1934. Its editor, William L. Crawford, put out several issues and hoped to attain a pro circulation for this combined sf-and-fantasy book. My first yarn appeared here . . . along with Schuyler Miller's 4-part serial, *The Titan*, and (oops, I told you so!)

David H. Keller, M.D., offering "The Golden Bough." The associated editors of *Marvel Tales* were Walter Dennis, who has gone on to distinguish himself, and one Lloyd A. Eshbach.

The next effort to hand is the December, 1934 issue of *The Fantasy Fan*, edited by Charles D. Hornig, who styles himself Managing Editor of *Wonder Stories*. It contains Lovecraft, Clark Ashton Smith, Robert Nelson and a particularly precious bit of Bloch, along with a column by Schwartz and Weisinger. Schwartz and Weisinger . . . there are two names to conjure with! (Say 'em often enough and you get rabbits out of hats.)

These two boys were also involved in *Fantasy Magazine* which boasted as the Literary Editor one Raymond A. Palmer, and as Fantascience Film Editor somebody named Forest A. Jackerman, — or some such name. The issue of *Fantasy* I have here contains material by these boys . . . and believe it or not, Messrs. Schwartz and Weisinger showed up in Philadelphia in 1953. It gave me a great thrill to see those venerable men pounding on the floor with their canes and waving their false teeth about with all the enthusiasm of a vigorous childhood.

In 1936 they had already attained the dignity of a 38th issue, featuring material by Eando Binder, Jack Williamson, Edmond Hamilton, Raymond Z. Gallun, John Russell Fearn, H. G. Wells, Walter Gillings, Festus Pragnell, Stanley Weinbaum, Raymond A. Palmer, Robert E. Howard, George Allan England, Clay Ferguson, Jr., Forrest J Ackerman and yours truly, who was doing an alleged column of alleged humor.

And here's a companion to *Marvel Stories*, called *Unusual Stories*. Winter, 1935, and it contains a poem by one Robert W. Lowndes. Meanwhile a young friend of his named Donald A. Wollheim was editing *The Phantagraph*, the last line of which reads as follows: "Is STF in a Rut? Left Out Till Next Issue."

There's a question for you. *Is* STF in a rut, in this, the year of our Lord, 1935? I dunno . . . I never got the next issue.

Come to think of it, as I peruse these early offerings with their Lovecraft, Howard, Clark Ashton Smith items and frequent references to Poe and Bierce, I am forcibly reminded that fantasy was given equal or greater consideration than "STF" in those days. In early 1937, David A. Kyle was putting out *Phantasy World*, alias *Fantasmagoria*, dedicated to H. P. Lovecraft and apparently hand-printed by a victim of *paralysis agitans* on the back of some used cleansing-tissue. Science came first in the title of the *Science-Fantasy Correspondent*, but it features, heaven forbid, a something called "A Visit with H. P. Lovecraft." The 'science' is largely evident in a scholarly article by Ackerman, entitled "Will Color Kill Fantascience Films?" The writer fears that this might well be the case . . . a pity he didn't stick around long enough to see *Destination Moon* or *When Worlds Collide* or some of the later efforts.

Comes now a rash of *Bloomington News Letters* and *Voms* and such-like manifestations of the early Forties. These were the days of West Coast Fandom. Through the pages of *The Acolyte* and *Madge* and *Chanticleer* and *The Fantasite* parade the names of Francis T. Laney, Samuel D. Russell, Duane W. Rimel, Carlton J. Fassbeinder, Milton A. Rothman (apparently you had to have a middle initial to get into the act). Tucker is largely in evidence here and so is Burbee, Warner, Liebscher, Carison, Joquel, Daugherty, Tigrina, Ashley (what — many of you don't remember these names? These were BNFs of just eight short years ago! Apparently sf moves faster than the speed of light).

Agenbite of Inwit, very arty, by Lowndes, in '45. And now the names grow recognizable: in 1945's *Grotesque*, edited by Judy Zissman, a young fan name of Larry Shaw explains the mysteries of silk screening, a Jim Blish writes about viruses as possible zombies. Here's 1949-50 with *New Purposes*, edited by Fritz Leiber. Never heard of that one? Well, it existed. And Don Day's *Fanscient*, and *Fantastic Worlds* . . . these offer a startling contrast to the tone of early ones.

And now we're up to Sixth or at least Five-and-a-Halfish Fandom with the British invasion: *Slant*, *Hyphen*, *Peri*, etc — and the intimate magazines: *Quandry*, *Confusion*, etc. . . . plus the domestic crop, *SF Bulletin*, *Spaceship*, *Vega*, *Skyhook*, *Destiny*, *Fanwarp*, *Vanations* and so forth.

On the face of it, one might well believe great changes have been made, great strides taken in fan publications. There are more magazines today, there are more ambitious efforts running to a hundred pages or even greater lengths. There are such mighty organs of public opinion as *Oopsla!* for instance.

And yet I wonder.

Today I received in the mail a magazine which shall remain nameless and blameless. It contains material from prominent fans and prominent pros. It is well-designed, with handsome art work and even semi-legible reading content. It might easily be representative of the Fanzine of 1954.

In the back is an announcement of the next issue's line-up. The feature article, I see, will be "Is Science Fiction in a Rut?"

I think I know the answer to that one . . .

A WAY OF LIFE

Before me on my desk as I write these lines is a fan magazine from Fond du Lac, Wisconsin, some fifty-five miles away.

Next to it rests a fanzine from California; beneath it, another from Texas, and beneath that an offering from New York. Cheek-by-jowl is a product of Northern Ireland, another from England, one from Germany, a 'zine from Canada and yet another from Australia.

If you happen to be, as I am, a hardened fan with a softened brain, you may be inclined to comment, "So what? Almost anybody active in sf fandom is in touch with other fans from all over the world."

Well, sir, I agree with you. About everything except the "So what?" part, that is.

To me, after all these years, it's still a pretty amazing phenomenon. And a highly significant one.

When I started out as a professional writer, some eighty years ago — give or take a few years — one of the things that impressed me most was the fact that ever so often I'd get a fan-letter (or complaint as the case might be, and usually was) from a reader in Mexico, New Zealand or Southern Rhodesia. It seemed to me at the time that one of the greatest advantages of being a published author was the opportunity to communicate with people thousands of miles away.

At the same time a then youthful fan named Forrest J Ackerman was beating the drums for Esperanto, the Universal Language. One of his arguments was that establishment of a common tongue would facilitate communication and human relationships between people all over the world.

But what I didn't know, and what Ackerman didn't know, was that we had right at our fingertips one of the best means of establishing just such a general communication — in the form of sf and sf fanzines.

The result is heaped before me as I write. Today, the "internationally circulated" fan magazine is a commonplace. Teenagers in the wilds of the Midwest can and do exchange regular correspondence with teenagers in the wilds of Middlesex. (I choose this location deliberately, for the benefit of readers who like to see more sex in my writing.)

In those far-off times of which I speak, it was considered remarkable if a fan drove or hitchhiked his way a few hundred miles to visit other fans or attend a fan-gathering. Now, as we are all aware, a journey of many thousands of miles is almost a commonplace — like a meeting of old friends.

I am inclined to gush a bit about this, not because I am naïvely impressed with the power of the postal system, but because of the overall effect in terms of human relationships.

For untold years, leading statesmen and renowned public figures have deluged us with pious blah about "learning to know our fellow men." If only we could visualize the inhabitants of other countries as "human beings," sharers of the same hopes and fears and problems, it might mean the eventual end of war, etc. You know the pitch.

You, as a fan, ought to know the pitch. Because you've seen it in actual practice right here in our miniature world of fandom.

Through fanzines, and through correspondence you've come to know something about life in modern Belgium, the West Zone of Berlin, the steaming swamplands of Savannah, the decadent stews of Belfast. The doings of the London Circle, the affairs of the Melbourne SF Group, the latest mutterings from the Hermit of Hagerstown — all are today a matter of available common knowledge.

An anthropologist, ethnologist, or sociologist of the future in search of data on our contemporary manners and mores, could do well to research a current offering of fan magazines. As exemplars of present-day attitudes in all categories — geographical, chronological, financial — they offer almost unlimited data.

And talk about "democracy in action!" The variety (and vehemence) of opinions expressed on every subject under the sun is perhaps unparalleled anywhere else today.

It is a curious — and to me a saddening — thing that in recent years most magazines and newspapers generally circulated have largely ceased to be real "organs of personal opinion." That is to say, they seldom reflect any personal opinion save that of the editors and publishers. True, an angry letter, a crank document or a brief protest may find its place in the reader's columns, always balanced, you may have noticed, by other letters of high praise. But there is little opportunity offered for full-fledged, full-throttle controversial discussion.

Yet in our fanzines, pro meets con, constantly. And fan meets pro, and pros con fans, and fans attend cons, and pros write prose and — well, you get the idea. Everything and anything goes: there may be twenty or more pages of letters or essay articles in addition to editorial opinion. Sometimes it's callow, sometimes it's raucous, sometimes it's disjointed, sometimes it's vulgar but always it's a healthy phenomenon. And a surprisingly high percentage of what appears is a thoughtful effort to communicate and share viewpoints.

I hold no lofty beliefs in sf fanzines as leaders of the Literature of Protest. I would not presume to extrapolate to the point where I'd say that if everybody became a fan and started exchanging views with other fans, war would vanish from the earth and all of the ills of mankind, including Johnny Ray and athlete's foot, would be eliminated.

But I do presume to call your attention to the way in which our little minority group manages to operate; to the way in which a hobby has brought about the kind of international good-will, coöperation, and understanding which high-priced and high-pressure political propaganda, operating on generalized impersonal levels, has never been able to achieve.

It may well be that our diplomatic embassies all over the world should be required to stock current fanzines in their reception rooms: that, in place of white tie and tails, our ambassadors would be better off if they donned helicopter beanies.

For many years now, I've been mounting my soap-box at meetings, at conventions, in the pages of fanzines and even in prozines, to proclaim one simple statement — "Fans are people."

Certainly this isn't a very profound observation, and it shouldn't be too difficult to understand. As a matter of fact, a portion of the general public has gradually come to accept the truth of this observation. Formerly, outsiders usually pointed the finger of scorn at fans with the observation, "Dig that crazy mixed-up kid," or even, "Dig that crazy mixed-up adult."

But the phrase is *passé*, and so is the thought behind it. Despite the attitude of a die-hard minority, it's easy to observe that most people are becoming increasingly tolerant of fandom as a hobby and are willing to consider fans as individuals.

Surprisingly enough, the greatest resistance to this notion seems to come from the ranks of the fans themselves.

I reach this conclusion reluctantly, but the evidence is unmistakably apparent in the pages of all too many fanzines these days. It is most marked whenever fans have occasion to refer to BNFs.

Just what is a BNF? According to the learned authority Tucker, in his *Neo-Fan's Guide*:

The "Big Name Fan," the person who is well-known and who has made a solid reputation for himself. This is usually accomplished by participating in fannish affairs for a long while, or by publishing a superior fanzine, or by consistently writing or illustrating in a manner identified with quality, or by any number of ways which keeps your name before fandom in a responsible manner. The term "BNF" has to be earned, it can never be appropriated or purchased, nor conferred upon yourself or your friends.

In other words, a BNF attains his or her status through *performance*.

That is how we judge human beings — by their performance. Actions speak louder than words.

At least, almost everywhere except, apparently, in fandom. All too many fans, when considering this BNF matter, seem to forget the definition cited above. They seem to forget the performance factor. And that's why I hold that they are not judging their fellow-fans as *people*.

Now it is not my intention to imply that the term BNF is possessed of any signal merit in itself; it is not the equivalent of a knighthood, an honorary Ph.D. from a College of Mortuary Science, or a membership in the World's Most Exclusive After-Shaving Club. To be known as a BNF is not quite on a par with becoming a Thirty-Second-Degree Mason, a Grand Imperial Dragon of the Ku Klux Klan, or Chairman of the Board in a lumber factory. BNF is a complimentary term in our little sewing-circle, yes, but it means nothing except to a few other sew-and-sews.

I don't think it is a Sacred Honor, and I don't believe it should be jealously guarded, reserved for only a Select Few, and awarded on the basis of a three hour examination (written) for males and a three hour examination (physical) for females.

But I do think fandom is inclined to kick around the term until it is in danger of losing even a modicum of meaning; and this simply because fans aren't willing to evaluate other fans as *people*. And to gauge them, as people, on the basis of their actual *performance*.

Pick up a fanzine, almost any fanzine, and see how many references are made to BNFs. The woods, apparently, are full of them, and so is the woodwork. A few issues of a fanzine, a half dozen articles in the fanzines of other editors, and a fair number of letters circulated amongst prozine outlets or private correspondents seems to qualify an individual, in the minds of far too many fans, as a genuine BNF. Even though the individual in question may put out a run-of-the-mill 'zine; his "articles" may consist merely of reviewing other fanzines or gripes against prozines; and his correspondence more distinguished by invective rather than invention. Indeed, quality and quantity alike seem to be minor factors — what seems to matter is just how loudly and emphatically the fan states his adverse critical opinions.

As a result, we have self-styled and seemingly accepted BNFs who earn their apparent status merely by participating in feuds: we have BNFs whose choice of language and statement of opinion offer no value but shock-value: we have BNFs who have presumably arrived at this distinction merely by using a reverse-switch on the old "guilt-by-association" idea and associating themselves and their activities only with other BNFs.

But the criterion of worth, I respectfully submit, is in the value of services rendered. *Value*, not *volume*.

And once we re-appraise the BNFs in terms of value, in terms of actual performance and contributions to the fan-field, the ranks diminish quickly. It's very easy to separate the men from the boys.

Now let me hasten to add one thing: that "men from the boys" phrase is figurative and not literal. Nor does mere seniority mean anything in fandom; it's not necessarily length of time spent in the field that counts.

In my own personal estimate, people like Lee Hoffman, Dean Grennell, Walt Willis and Shelby Vick became BNFs in only a year or so of fanning, because of the tangible contributions they made to the field. Whereas it is possible (if not exactly polite) to name a good many people who have "been around" fandom for a half-dozen years or even longer, and who show no signs of ever being capable of attaining BNF status.

Now just what "tangible contributions" make a BNF? According to the broad terms of the Tucker definition almost all fan activity will enable an individual to qualify — if this activity is identifiable with "quality" and keeps your name before fandom "in a responsible manner."

Within the broad confines of the field, almost anyone can write, anyone can illustrate, anyone can publish, anyone can correspond, anyone can form a club or hold a so-called "convention" or start a so-called "movement." But when we consider the matter of *quality* and the degree of *responsibility* we can make a sound judgment.

It's not my purpose here to attempt to make a listing of all those who — in my opinion — are rightfully entitled to the designation of BNF. But I would, perhaps, help to illustrate the basic premise by citing a few examples.

In my opinion, then, I'd classify as BNFs all those who have made an effort to provide fandom with a written record — historical or definitive; who have attempted to give fandom a frame of reference and a sense of continuity. In this category one brings to mind Sam Moskowitz and his *Immortal Storm*, Jack Speer and the *Fancyclopedia*, the aforementioned Bob Tucker with his *Neo-Fan's Guide* and his *Fan-Survey*; also Don Day and his Index and (on a slightly more professional level) Messrs. Dikty and Bleiler with their compendium. If the people mentioned above had done absolutely nothing else within the field, these signal contributions would be enough to stamp them as true BNFs — even if they never once came out in the pages of *The Crudzine Quarterly* with a Fearless Letter pillorying Palmer, hamstringing Hamling, goading Gold or crucifying Campbell.

Similarly, I'd grant BNF status to everyone who has ever been a prime mover in putting on a successful regional or national convention. It's not necessarily the Chairmen I'm thinking of, either, but the *real* workers — whether or not they happen to hold titles. Oftentimes they aren't active in the editing-publishing aspect of fandom, but their contribution to the field as a whole is a major one. Dr. C. L. Barrett is, of course, a name that comes instantly to mind. Doc is certainly a BNF, although he has never put out a single copy of a 100-page Annish.

I'd also classify as BNFs those who, through the years, have demonstrated willingness to perform services over and above the call of duty in connection with furthering the growth and development of the various APAs. I am not thinking so much about the people who get their kicks from quibbling over "constitutions" and interpretations of "by-laws" as I am about fans who have held office in such organizations and stimulated real activity on the part of the membership. The same would hold true for the fan clubs throughout the nation.

In the field of actual fan-publication, I defer to Mr. Tucker with his reference to a "superior fanzine." Here again, quality and responsibility are the *criteria*; not quantity and volume. After a dozen years, people still remember (and, if they're fortunate enough to own copies, cherish) Laney's *The Acolyte*; Lee Hoffman's *Quandry* was and is a distinctive effort; an all-too-infrequent *Skyhook* from Redd Boggs is still worth a hundred issues of (*fill in your own choice, who needs trouble?*). That is not to say that it's impossible to make a valid contribution with frequent issues; certainly the *Fantasy-Times* offers ample demonstration to the contrary.

The same, I think, holds true in the matter of writing *for* fanzines. Bob Silverberg's famous piece of a few years back which resulted in the still-disputed birth of a still-disputed Seventh Fandom is a case in point: there had been nothing to equal its effect since Dr. Frankenstein created his monster. Consistently good writing — serious or facetious, sf-oriented or devoted to other interests — can make a BNF. Take a look at Harry Warner, or Dean Grennell, or the work of many contributors to 'zines such as *Inside*, *Psychotic* or *Oopsla!* for further evidence.

But in this connection, let me once again emphasize the fact that fanzines, while they are a fairly accurate mirror, lack the scope to reflect the *entire* aspect of fandom. It is possible (as in the case of Dr. Barrett) to become a BNF without ever editing, publishing or writing for a fan magazine. I stress this merely because it is in the pages of fanzines that one generally comes across the distorted notions of what constitutes BNF status.

Let me repeat, at the risk of reiterated redundancy (to say nothing of alarming alliteration) you don't get to be a genuine BNF just by spreading your name around and getting people to know you. There's a lot of difference between mere notoriety and real recognition.

In a sense, as I tried to say when I started out, all this is very unimportant. Since the term BNF carries with it no tangible reward and no actual prestige save in a very minor field, it can quite easily be dismissed as being of no consequence, no matter to whom it is applied.

But on the other hand, fandom does have a value as a cross-section of human relationships. Many a youngster has grown up (and, let us hope, many more will grow up) in the field. The friendships they cultivate there, the experiences they undergo, and the judgments about effort, worth and rewards they make as a result of what they find in fandom renders it important that we emphasize the difference between mere labels and actual performance. It is important, too, that we all realize that becoming a BNF is not the end-all or be-all of fanactivity. There are plenty of people around who don't necessarily want to become Big Wheels — they're quite happy merely to go along for a pleasant ride. As such, they're more than welcome, and their company is more appreciated; fandom is the kind of vehicle that moves better with a full load of passengers, and there's no need to expect that everyone must serve as a conductor or engineer; sheer interest is ticket enough for the trip. Our only dispute is with those who claim a place in the engineer's cab without really helping to stoke the boiler — they blow a loud whistle, but they don't get us anywhere; and I'd better drop the analogy right now before we end up on the wrong track.

* * * * *

The year is still young as these lines are being written, and I haven't seen the article yet.

But it will come, never fear.

It always comes, every year, with the infallibility of a swallow returning to Capistrano or disappearing down an editor's throat.

Those of you who have inhabited the merry microcosm of fandom for a while will know what article I mean. But you neo-fans will be surprised — and perhaps shocked — when you read it. And that's precisely the reason why I'd like to anticipate the article in advance this year.

The article I refer to will appear in one of the fanzines, and it will be couched in strong and scathing language. It will be written by a fan seething with sarcastic indignation, and will take the form of an announcement that this fan is leaving fandom because he has "grown up."

Now this matter of dropping out of fandom is neither unusual nor reprehensible. Tastes and habits do change, and personal circumstances frequently arise which make active participation in a hobby unfeasible. Every year, certain fans quietly take their leave, while new fans arrive and pitch their tents on the sites vacated by the silent departing Arabs.

But the person who will write the article I have in mind is neither silent nor Arabian. He is bound and determined that his passing marks the world's end, and he intends to make surc that the ending comes with a big bang rather than a loud whimper.

He isn't content to go his way in peace. He must first compose a personal manifesto, to the effect that he has seen the Error of his Ways and is Repenting. With a truly religious fervor, he will infer that fandom is made up of Miserable Sinners: that its interests and occupations are callow, shallow, juvenile, imbecile. He will cite chapter and verse in an effort to bolster up his case; he will piously lament that "presumably intelligent people" still "waste their time" editing or contributing to fanzines, reading sf, attending meetings or conventions. He will urge them to awake to Reality and the Big World Outside, and generously offer them a glimpse of his mature outlook in contrast to the petty preoccupations of fandom.

Often he will "confess" his errors in precisely the same manner as an ex-Communist will upon embracing Democracy — or, for that matter, like a practicing Communist who recants a now outmoded "party line" of ideology.

Big deal.

Now I'm in no position to state just how many people have been influenced in the past by such dramatic denunciations and departures. I suspect very few fans have actually abandoned their hobby because of the urgings of the disaffected.

But since it's obvious enough that we don't live in a world of utter black-and-white values, sometimes the remarks of a departing fan do call our attention to a bit of tattle-tale gray in the field. And it's possible that many of us, in our more sober and reflective moments, allow a few doubts to creep in concerning the values and benefits of fandom as a hobby.

We listen to the criticism and reflect that some of it seems to have a basis in truth. There *are* some offbeat characters in fandom (present company not necessarily excepted). There have been some regrettable incidents and irregularities. Petty feuds are not unknown. Some fans are fanatic and seemingly harbor delusions of grandeur concerning the importance of the field and/or their position in it.

And certainly, as a self-constituted minority group, fans are constantly subject to external pressure and ridicule from the self constituted majority groups who insist *their* hobbies are more important because more people share them. This "mathematical proof" reasoning may or may not echo in our psyches when doubt creeps in.

But before we bow to the dictates of the majority, and of the article-writer who has made this Great Discovery that fandom is only a trivial hobby, perhaps we ought to consider a few of the benefits accruing to fan activity.

Elsewhere I have had occasion to dwell at length (and rent-free, too!) on the notion that fandom is a valuable source of contact in making friends. No need to sharpen the point; most of us who have spent time in the field continue to do so because we *have* made friends. We enjoy sharing our hobby, our interests, and even our social life with people of similar congenial tastes. The delight of communication, on an international basis, is available to the fan editor, contributor or correspondent.

But such an argument, of course, won't satisfy the disenchanted critic. He will continue to insist, in effect, that fandom is merely a glorified waste of time. He won't listen to sentimental opinions. He wants facts and figures.

So be it.

Exactly what material benefit can a fan derive from his participation in fandom?

Let's look at the record.

If you harbor any ambition to become a writer, illustrator, editor, or publisher, there is no easier avenue of approach to your goal than the field of science fiction fandom.

Since the day when teen-age fan Charles D. Hornig was plucked directly from fannish ranks and plunked into the editorial seat of a professional sf magazine, these "success stories" abound.

Without any pretense of being comprehensive or all-inclusive in my listing, allow me to offer a few examples that come readily to mind.

Amongst writers, we find the names of James Blish, who hectographed (in a manner to bring howls of horror from today's conscientious editors) a crude little fanzine when in his early teens. We can list young Poul Anderson, juvenile Henry Kuttner — who used to write letters to *Weird Tales* — and a kid named damon knight. Let's not forget little Freddie Pohl, or a gal named Judy Zissman, who now writes under the name of Judith Merril. And then there's Fritz Leiber, Joe Gibson and Cyril Kornbluth and a brash young punk, who used to hang around the LASFS, whose name was Bradbury. Artists like Hannes Bok and Virgil Finlay were fans long before they began their professional careers. Forrest Ackerman, Julius Schwartz, Oscar J. Friend are remembered as fans in the days when they couldn't possibly hope to become agents, since they were unable to figure out 10% of any given amount.

A writer like Wilson Tucker, with a dozen books to his credit, is still better-known today as Bob Tucker in fannish circles. And there are a host of transitional figures — fans who are currently establishing themselves as professional writers with mounting sales. A few easily brought to awareness in this connection: Jim Harmon, Bob Silverberg, Vernon L. McCain, Dean R. Grennell, Dave Mason, Marion Zimmer Bradley, the immortal Lou Tabakow and Harlan Ellison.

Editors? Robert W. Lowndes and Donald Wollheim were prominent early fans. Larry Shaw, Donald A. Wollheim, Raymond A. Palmer, Beatrice Mahaffey, Sam Moskowitz, Jerry Bixby and Bill Hamling. All of them cut their eye-teeth on fanactivity.

Fantasy and science fiction publishers? Lloyd Eshbach, Melvin Korshak, Martin Greenberg — publishing the works of such fans-turned-pro as E. E. Evans, Basil Wells, Frank Robinson. The name of Ted Dikty comes to mind here, as does that of Judy May Dikty. And then there's Oliver Saari, Earl Kemp, Chad Oliver, Les Cole, Lester del Rey; and just about *everybody* in England seems to turn up sooner or later in their magazines. Willis, Shaw, Harris, Bulmer, Tubb, Campbell, Turner — right on down the line, they go from fanactivity to writing and editing and illustrating and publishing in natural sequence and progression.

And if we extend our concept of fanactivity to include avid and continuous readers in the medium, we'll have to let just about every other "big name" in the field into our category. Almost without exception, they've been readers from 'way back; and if they live, or lived, in metropolitan areas they were regular attendees at fan club meetings and conventions too.

No doubt about it: there are benefits to be found in this hobby of ours, and material benefits at that. Of course, there is no pretense made that one can necessarily make a fortune in the field, but on the other hand, how much cash does the average baseball fan or wrestling devotee ever derive from pursuing his hobby? And where is the Arthur C. Clarke of the bowling world — a field in which one cannot even hope to make pin-money?

It is difficult to name a single established writer, editor or regular contributor to the professional sf magazines who has not done his or her share of "fanning" at one time or another — and derived benefits therefrom. Possibly the sole exception is our good friend "Doc" Smith. He was not a fan when he was young, because there were no fanzines in those days — printing hadn't been invented yet. But you probably know he makes up for the lack today, and is a devoted convention attendee.

So much for the record. In itself it offers eloquent rebuttal to the claims that fandom offers nothing of material value to the hobbyist. And as for *other*, more important values, you can answer that question for yourself.

It goes without saying that not every fan is going to establish a career as a professional — nor, in the majority of instances, is such a goal even contemplated. But the opportunity is there. And so is the pleasure and reward of participation for its own sake.

EVERY MAN HIS OWN PSYCHIATRIST

or, Is There A Doctor On The Couch?

This is Psychiatry's Golden Age. Everywhere we turn there are ladies in the dark; we stumble into snake-pits, unaFreud, for our hearts are Jung and gay. Evidence of amateur analysis is everywhere at hand. Pick up the newspaper and read the crime reports; the homocidal are now identified as homosexual, the cat burglar is labeled a catatonic. Switch on the radio. Young Doctor Malone is giving John's Other Wife a sample of the cathartic method, thus tying in neatly with the laxative commercial at the end of the program. The screen is filled with bearded character actors who gravely advise delinquent young heroes to go West where men are Menninger. Every drama has its trauma; neuroses are read and if Violet is blue she is probably a manic-depressive. In our police courts, methodology has been brought up to date — the drunk who formerly got a urinalysis now gets a psychoanalysis.

It is no wonder, then, that inhibition begets exhibition — no wonder that personal disturbances once regarded as a pack o' trouble are now looked upon as a peccadillo. Self-analysis is the order, or the disorder of the day. Men and women rush around setting up hastily improvised confessional booths to the tune of "You Tell Me Your Dream and I'll Tell You Mine."

During the past several years, scores of friends, acquaintances and near-strangers have beaten a path to my door and then beaten down the door in an effort to climb up on my couch and regale me with a *nocturne*. Everybody wants to discuss dreams, although couches have other uses.

Since I am by no means the only person in the world owning a couch, I feel fairly certain that this is a widespread condition.

At first, however, I was slightly aghast at a guest who guessed he'd gas about his ghastly *geas*. Everybody insisted on talking about dreams — including the insomniacs.

Elderly women of the haughtiest *haute monde* have spoken to me about the most intimate details of their subconscious. It is a bit disconcerting to hear grandma tell you about how she identifies the gorilla as the minister of the First Congregational Church. Sweet young virgins have recounted sexual exploits with purple alligators; neat, subdued housewives have launched into hour-long rambling dissertations on their dreams in accents more fecal than fickle.

It is getting so that I half expect to hear such unburdenings from strangers on the bus or streetcar; I *do* hear them regularly from the person standing next to me at a bar.

There seems to be neither shame nor reticence when it comes to discussing what happens in a dream. Sleep has become the great national alibi — anything goes as long as one slumbers; anything from somnambulism to enuresis.

Recognizing these truths, I am no longer shocked when the cleaning lady drops the mop and begins to tell me about the dream where she jumped over a series of candles, umbrellas, church steeples and Washington Monuments in an effort to catch up with her daughter in foetal form. I merely whip out a false beard, adjust it quickly to my chin and hope to heaven it will hide my smirk.

I smirk because it's all a fake. The unburdening, the opening of soul and sewer — meaningless and absurd. Everyone will tell you his dreams, but no one will tell you what is actually a much greater source of self-revelation . . . his *daydreams*.

For sleep, as I remarked, is the great national alibi. It is the excuse, the extenuation. But the daydream —

So far I have been unsuccessful in soliciting a single solitary daydream from any of the bold, free, scientific-minded souls who offer the unaesthetic products of their anaesthesia. Many of them, in fact, actually refuse to admit they have *daydreams*.

"None of your business" . . . "Think I'm crazy?" . . . "Don't have time for such silliness" . . . "Only kids have daydreams."

This attitude is in itself evidence of the relatively greater importance of the daydream as a clue to personality. The element of conscious cognition implicit in the daydream is of vital concern to the *psyche-plumbers*. From the daydream springs the Messianic delusion, the Hitler, the hatchet-fiend, the nympholept.

While the boys with the goatees analyze, interpret, abstract and just plain guess their way through the symbolic and semantic maze of sleep; while they attempt to look at the teeth and withers of a nightmare, they largely ignore a horse of a different choler.

The daydream is naked, unashamed, self-evident. As a matter of fact, the free-fantasy and free-association techniques have been developed in an effort to stimulate the very sort of self-admission which has the daydream as its embodiment. The wishes, impulses, sexual berations and aberrations which can be uncovered only after painful months of "dream interpretation" with the aid of *Uncle Sig's Gypsy Dream Book* are readily available in the actual conscious content of the diurnal fantasy.

Sometimes I imagine a world in which everyone dispenses with hypocrisy and pretense, shame and subterfuge, fraud and affectation — where one speaks of one's private thoughts and wishes freely and without constraint. How much of human misery and strife would be eradicated if only this were possible? But — that's a daydream, too.

THIS METHOD OF CATHARSIS

To me (and to my little-known collaborator, a man name of Sigmund Freud) there are only two primary writer-motivations: namely, ego-gratification and catharsis. You can combine ego-gratification and catharsis in one object by picturing an enema tube with your name printed on it.

Seriously, though, I think all writer-motivation analysis must be approached from these two angles.

The ego-gratification phase is, I think, self-evident. There is ample evidence in the pages of any promag . . . of the guy who writes a yarn to demonstrate his amazing knowledge or facile cleverness. In fantasy, there's the guy who wants to gain a sort of perverted recognition by shocking his readers (as a kid, you met the same guys at a boys' camp; they were the ones who talked at the dinner table about eating loathsome concoctions). There is the guy who Utopiayarns in order to make the reader identify him as a profound thinker and a leader . . . the guy who writes in an absurdly brusque fashion in order to underplay normal emotional reactions and appear ultra-sophisticated. And, of course, since every author writes for readers, applause is the object, ego-gratification the obvious key to his work.

But . . . this method of catharsis . . .

Now, I am highly tempted to illustrate what I mean by "analyzing" the cathartic element in the work of a number of contemporary writers. I believe I can detect the obvious confessional element of several fantasy producers. But that would be vastly unfair. I must therefore limit myself to the cathartic material in my own yarns . . . dreary as the process may be.

Between the ages of seventeen and twenty-eight (1935-45), I published about 125 fantasy yarns. Let's ignore the ego-gratification and concentrate on catharsis. During the years 1935-38, I wrote stories about Egypt, about Druids and a number of pseudo Lovecraftian tales. A casual survey would imply that I wanted to demonstrate my knowledge of Egyptology and Druidism (which is very shabby and limited) and that I wished to imitate the work of the master.

But that's a mistake — considering motivation in terms of the story-content. Here's where catharsis comes in. Ignore "what is the story *about* ?" Ignore the style. Concentrate on what lurks beneath the surface. Consider character and setting.

What kind of heroes does the author use? Do they triumph or do they fail? What qualities cause them to triumph or fail? What settings are employed? What villains or personifications of evil are utilized? These are the questions for cathartic analysis. Use them on my yarns for the period 1935-38 and see what happens.

My "heroes" or protagonists (for the "hero" is often the villain) are either beaten-down scholars who blunder into trouble and are destroyed, or mercenary rats who blunder into trouble and are destroyed. They seek . . . and find only death.

Youthful cynicism . . . adolescent preoccupation with the problems of the depression where the poor scholar (that's me, folks) fails . . . and the smug realist also fails (that's a wish-fulfillment fantasy, folks). In other words, the philosophy of defeat implicit . . . "Why seek, you only get into trouble anyway."

Obvious stuff, eh? Any kid can do it? Now, let's get cathartic. In virtually every story I wrote between 1935 and 1938, the villain or evil or doom lurked *underground*.

Underground . . . that's where evil lurks. At the same time, that's where the treasure lies. That's where the hero goes. Seeking treasure, finding doom.

Get out your Freud, folks.

Can't you see the adolescent, subconsciously obsessed with the female sexual regions ? Underground . . . treasure . . . possible danger and doom . . . mystery . . .

Now we're getting somewhere. That's what I was writing about, whether I knew it or not. Sexual symbolism. Shades of *Jurgen*!

At this time I pause to realize that if I were to proceed from 1938 onward, I would get increasingly tangled up in a dozen additional symbolic references which enter from that point. It would stretch this pleasant little exercise out for fifteen pages or so, and to what end?

Let other, more qualified intellects take up the torch from here . . . take up the torch and set fire to the whole damned thing, for all of me.

But at least I don't write about caverns so much any more!

THEM AIN'T BONGO DRUMS

. . . That's Opportunity Knocking!

While browsing through the pages of a men's magazine the other day and admiring the advertisements for black lace panties and Freudian slips, it suddenly occurred to me that fandom is neglecting a great opportunity.

This opportunity, I hasten to assure you, has nothing to do with black lace panties (if it did, I wouldn't be fool enough to tell *you* about it!). But the aforesaid men's magazine — in fact, all magazines during the past year or so — have been crammed full of articles, essays, critical comment and free publicity for something called the Beat Generation.

Now when it comes to fandom, I'm as loyal as the next guy (a very pale fellow with pink eyes who tells me he's Carl Brandon's albino brother) and I have only our best interests at heart. As you probably know, I'm a member of FAPA, and a holder of an N3F trophy (which I put down only when I go to the bathroom). So my great suggestion, which I am about to make as soon as I can remember just what in hell it is, is intended in a spirit of constructive criticism.

Briefly, it is this: Why not let fandom replace the Beat Generation?

If you're inclined to think this suggestion farfetched, let me reassure you on that point; I got it without ever having to stir from this typewriter.

Let us consider the facts, if any.

Up until a couple of years ago, the Beatniks were almost totally unknown. Kerouac and Ginsberg were nonentities; Rexroth and Patchen had been around for years without anybody giving them a tumble. Then all at once the deluge of publicity started and the panic was on. The Beat Generation became a craze, a topic of conversation and — more important — a commercial vehicle. Obscure writers and poets were elevated to financial eminence overnight, and on what basis? A couple of books about hitchhiking around the country and a few bits of poetry recited against a background of refrigerated jazz and a bongo beat.

Now, as is inevitable with any fad, the Beatnik kick is passing. Give it another six months to a year at most and it will be dead. By the time all the sack dresses will have been cut up into dust-rags and the hula hoops transformed into earrings for Zsa Zsa Gabor, the whole Beat Generation bit will vanish from public consciousness and something new will replace it.

Why shouldn't *we* take over?

We've got all the necessary ingredients. If critics can get so steamed up about cross country travelogs, why won't they flip for something like *The Harp Stateside*? Of course, Willis would have to rewrite it and set it up a bit — but this would merely mean that he'd put in some reminiscences he was gallant enough to omit in the original version. Why, a dozen other fans could follow suit with their own uncensored reports of fan-gatherings and fanac and visits to fan-clubs and homes. They could turn out stuff that would make *On The Road* read like a detour.

And when it comes to the artistic routine; is there any reason why fan-poets like Randall Garrett couldn't learn to recite their stuff to a musical accompaniment? This of the potential LP record sales in our midst! I can hear it now, in stereophonic sound — Tony Boucher and Poul Anderson reciting dirty limericks against a bongo beat, with paradiddles on the punch-lines! Some of the stuff I've heard at conventions would make Ginsberg's *Howl* sound like a thin bleat.

Then we've got the art bit; Rotsler and ATom and all the rest could turn out *genre* material. And fandom as a whole can offer a backlog of written material roughly ten thousand times greater than has been produced by the entire beat school of writers (and I do mean roughly).

Let's not forget the revised *Fancyclopedia*, either. Part of the charm of the Beatnik approach has resided in their vocabulary . . . but this pitiful, meagre collection of words and phrases borrowed largely from musicians who aren't half as quick on the uptake as they are fast on a fix just doesn't begin to compare with the large and picturesque fannish vernacular. Why should the general public be content to mouth such unappetizing words as "bugged" and "dragged" when they can announce to the world at large that they're "going gafia" . . . who flips, man? Not when you can go Sercon! Oh, we've *got* the vocabulary, no doubt about it!

And as for types — we've got the fannish characters who can back the Beatniks right off the map. Even the costumes are right for it; there must be a hundred fans all set to pose picturesquely for *Life* and *Look*. Have beard, will travel. . . .

That leather-jacket and dirty-jeans outfit will never begin to compare with what fandom could offer . . . the propellor beanie! It could become a national craze overnight (and if it does, that is the night I stay home in bed).

But seriously, it *could* happen. Somebody, some time, sooner or later, is going to do a *real* novel on fandom. Dave Ish did a story for an *avant garde* collection; I've done tongue-in-cheek or hole-in-head pieces on how fandom could take over the world — or, conversely, go underground as a persecuted minority. The full-scale novel is inevitable, and it could just possibly (with proper promotion; or better still, improper promotion) start the ball rolling. With Ackerman handling the publicity and Dave Kyle telling the critics where they could sit, we might be on our way. The Beatnik Brigade could be *big*!

It's worth thinking about. All we really have to do is point our heads in the right direction. I suggest we call a special meeting at the edge of the Grand Canyon, get behind this thing, and push.

On with the beanies — revv propellers!

CHILDREN OF BLUNDER

During the Christmas season, a full-page ad appeared in a Milwaukee newspaper which presumably made a simultaneous showing all over the country. It offered a **JET ROCKET SPACE SHIP 7 FEET LONG — SEATS 2-5, ONLY $4.98!**

The copy, written in glowing hucksterese, described the delights of "The Most Sensational Toy in America," artfully stressing the "educational value" for the benefit of the parents. Calling attention to the government's announcement of a forthcoming earth satellite, they remark that this is only the first step toward the conquest of space. But, they add, "the toymakers have beaten the scientists . . . the youngsters can conquer space right now."

A more direct message went to the kiddies themselves. Here's a partial quote:

". . . with all your jet and rocket-firing equipment in action, you BLAST OFF! You set your course, steering with the directional jets at the stern which are controlled by separate throttles at your fingertips. Your forward disintegrator guns go into action. Your fully-equipped radar instrument panel shows the target! You release your load of powerful nuclear bombs and bullseye! You return home victoriously, set your reversing mechanism and you're in for a quick landing. This is just an idea of all the wonderful things you can do with your sensational new Space Ship. Acclaimed for its educational value. Stimulates imagination . . ."

Ah, yes. What could be more educational, more stimulating to our kiddies, than the thought of operating a dandy space ship that can not only reach other planets but immediately drop nuclear bombs on them! What better training for the future could our youngsters possibly enjoy? What toy could be as completely modern and realistic as this, and yet convey the full spirit of our civilization and its outlook? To say nothing of the true spirit of Christmas? (At the time of writing, Americans had not yet celebrated the birthday of their chief Deity with the human sacrifice of 600-plus accident victims.)

For some years now, as a writer of horror stories and novels about psychopaths, I have been constantly confronted with certain attitudes on the part of my readers. Summed up, they amount to:

"How can you possibly dream up such awful ideas and such wicked characters?"

It has been my custom to explain that I am careful, in my writing, to stress the fact that my characters are aberrated, that their ideas and actions in no way reflect a normal outlook and that "the opinions expressed in this story are not necessarily those of the author."

But my readers, or at least a certain portion of them, continue to give me a fishy stare by way of reply, and some of them come right out and say that where there's smoke, there's fire — and anyone who is capable of thinking up such hideous notions must be a bit of a monster.

All this I endure, in return for a few paltry dollars.

Or did endure, until I read the advertisement mentioned here. Now my eyes are opened.

Why should I waste my time and effort transcribing my psycho-pathological fantasies to paper — for meager pennies and liberal abuse — when I could win both fame and fortune by translating realities to cardboard, instead?

Nobody, to my knowledge, has gone around protesting to the manufacturers of this "Space Ship" because it turns out to be a toy atomic-bombing unit. Perhaps I ought to heed this cue and follow suit. Instead of pandering to the morbidity of the adult population, I should appeal to the strong sense of reality and social consciousness of the kiddies.

Unfortunately, Christmas has come and gone.

But next Christmas looms ahead. If I use that as a target date and get to work right now, perhaps I can devise a few little cardboard toy-kits that will have a similar "educational appeal."

At the moment, my funds are limited. But surely there will be some among you who will realize the enormous sales-potential here, and join me in this enterprise with funds sufficient to pay for manufacturing and advertising costs.

Here's what I have in mind.

This "Space Ship" notion is magnificent, granted. But it still has a *touch* of the fantastic about it; even the ad-writers must strain a point when they endeavor to show that such a toy really "educates" a child for a possible future.

I believe it is possible to take the same amount of cardboard and give the children an equal amount of pleasure, without departing from reality one bit. I have in mind a few kits that are truly "educational" in every sense of the word, and yet packed with fun for healthy youngsters.

For example, there's my SEGREGATION KIT, which includes a cardboard schoolhouse and a cardboard schoolbus, complete with Jim Crow section in the rear. It has a piece of burnt cork, to be applied to the victim; a genuine leather whip (for the same purpose) and a full 15 feet of good hemp rope, featuring a pre-tied hangman's knot. The *de luxe* model could also include a small bucket of tar, a package of feathers and several sheets with eye-holes.

This should be a big regional seller during next year's Christmas shopping season.

For national distribution, there's the handsome new SPEEDWAY OUTFIT, consisting of a cardboard Cadillac, a plastic motorcycle and a great big mock-up ambulance, roomy enough to hold four "victims." Harmless sheets of transparent rock candy, such as are used in motion pictures, can be installed as window glass in the cars and broken during "accidents." A more expensive model would include several realistic dummy "victims." The same principle which enables dolls to "wet" can be applied to make these dummies "bleed" during and after the collisions.

As a profitable sideline, one might sell driving costumes — the black, metal-studded uniforms and Storm Trooper boots for the motorcyclist and a false stomach and harmless rubber cigar for the "executive type" in the Cadillac. Since the Space Ship includes an Astro-Star Map, this outfit might well include a Driver's Cursing Manual with which the kiddies could learn to impart realism. On second thought, this is probably unnecessary — most of them have listened to Daddy when he gets out on the highway.

For older children, interested in mathematics, there's my BUSINESS MAN'S KIT, which contains actual Income Tax Blanks, with instructions on how to fill them out falsely: a fake "Expense Account," a dummy Corporation Set-Up and a complete cardboard courtroom.

This may sound pretty tame alongside of Space Ships — but then, we've got a duty toward the younger generation. We must prepare them to face reality. And not all of them will be able to fulfill Man's Highest Destiny and go out to drop bombs on the stars.

So they might as well learn to content themselves with the simple pleasures within the reach of all — and stimulate their imaginations as best they can, playing "grown-up."

Still, perhaps, today's youngsters will not willingly settle for less than the ultimate in modern, scientific play-equipment. And I sometimes wonder how Dickens would rework his *Christmas Carol* if he were penning it today.

I rather think we'd find Tiny Tim perched on the shoulders of sturdy Bob Cratchit, just as in the old tale — but no longer would he lisp his hackneyed "God bless us, every one!" Instead, like a true child of his times, he would lean forward and drop a cardboard weapon on a cardboard city, with the joyous shout of "Bombs Away!"

HOW WEAK WAS MY END

Doctor Barrett, that eminent veterinarian of Bellefontaine, Ohio, had invited Bloch down to the annual Midwest Fan Conference for three years running.

But Bloch refused to run . . . he waited until he got a lift in an automobile. Came May of 1952, and one Oliver Saari of Chicago was seduced into providing transportation. And so it was off to Indian Lake for a weekend of fun, frolic and fandom. "Grin and Barrett" was the motto pasted on Bloch's valise. — Off through Illinois, Indiana and Ohio to Beastley's-On-The-Lake Hotel.

Bestials Indian Fake Resort is a big summer hotel adjoining the lake and bordering on the ridiculous. Upon arrival, Bloch and his extinguished companions found approximately 100 fans, editors, authors, publishers and hucksters huddled in the corridors in an effort to keep warm. After a light lunch (consisting of two 75-watt bulbs) Bloch retired to his room to rest up from the trip.

There is an old burlesque routine involving a honeymoon couple in a hotel room, where their efforts to retire are periodically interrupted by a maniac, a man with a bass drum, a bellboy, a troop of Boy Scouts and a detachment of bird watchers.

What happened to Bloch would make Gypsy Rose Lee turn over in her g-string. Here's the situation. Sitting on his bed with a cover pulled over his valise; unarmed save for a glass of scotch, is Bloch. Enter, in the order of their appearance (how else?):

Bea Mahaffey, she takes a glass and sits on Bloch's feet.

Pat Mahaffey, sister to Bea, she takes a glass and part of Bloch's blanket.

Virginia Saari, wife of Oliver, she takes a glass and the other side of Bloch's blanket.

Mack Reynolds, a simple goat-herder from Taos, New Mexico. He takes a glass and one look at Bloch and says, "My gawd, you work fast!"

Marty Greenberg and Dave Kyle, they take glasses and seats at the bedside.

Wilson Tucker, who gives Bloch a Los Angeles-type greeting, then gets off the bed and sits down.

Lee Hoffman, a constructed rebel, she gets the dressing-table bench and a glass.

There were others — in and out. Other people, other glasses, other bottles. Other voices, other rooms.

Meanwhile, there was some kind of Convention going on somewhere. Bloch, going through the lobby for supper, encountered a welter of celebrities. Milling through the corridors and spilling through the glassware were groups from Illinois, Indiana, Ohio, Pennsylvania, Michigan, Georgia, Florida, New York — plus one specimen that had just flown out of Carlsbad Caverns at dusk. Night reeled and fell and the group arranged itself in the lobby for the first official step in what turned out to be the *Tuckercon*.

Wilson TUCKER, Illinois fan, had brought some slides which were projected by Bob TUCKER. A running commentary on the slides was provided by W. Arthur TUCKER.

Following the slides came a sound-recorder drama written and produced for *Tucker Enterprises* by Wilson A. TUCKER.

Then TUCKER auctioned off some originals — only to return to the projection machine and set up some slides from England. A Mr. Arthur C. Clarke assisted him by making a few comments.

By this time it was close to 11 P.M. with barely eight hours left for a short poker game before bedtime. The particular poker game that Bloch attended was held by Wilson "Bob" TUCKER — in Bloch's room.

After the game, and a refreshing half-hour of sleep, it was suddenly Sunday noon and time for the banquet. The main course turned out to be chicken limbs, fried in rich golden-brown axle grease.

Doc Barrett then mounted his podium and began to introduce people like crazy — among them, a Mr. TUCKER, whose tape-recorder was spinning merrily. No doubt *Tucker Publications Inc.* will edit the tape and present it at the official *Tuckercon* in the city of Cituckergo in Septuckerember.

Once the banquet was over and everyone was tuckered out, the entire gathering seemed to dissipate rapidly. It was one of the most dissipated gatherings Bloch had ever seen. When the smoke cleared away, no one was left but Doc Barrett, Doc and Mrs. Smith, Bea, Judy, Ollie, Virginia, Dikty and Bloch . . . plus an unidentified fan named B-- T-----. After supper it was decided there was no reason for having all that smoke cleared away, so a fire was built in Tucker's room under a poker table. Contributions were made to the *Tucker Research Foundation*.

Next day it was farewell to Beastley's. As the last firecracker fell into the lake, the deserted hotel corridors stood forlorn and empty and a single bat fluttered into the belfry. . . .

Meanwhile, with only 100 days to go, Bloch is starting to get into training for Labor Day.

HOW TO ATTEND A SCIENCE FICTION CONVENTION

or, The Manly Art of Self-Defense

I am a little boy thirty-five years of age, but already I have attended four sf conventions. Or, rather, two conventions and two long parties with George O. Smith.

As I sit here in the peaceful twilight of my iron lung and muse back through the years, I contemplate those affairs and endeavor to collect my thoughts — which isn't as easy as it sounds, if you have two heads. If you don't, then this won't interest you anyway.

But let's say, for the sake of argument (and we must have arguments, or what would be the sense of holding a convention in the first place?) that you're a typical, red-blooded American two-headed sf fan, with a double beanie.

And let us further assume that the coming convention will be the first you'll ever attend. Lucky, lucky you! Think of the fun, the glamour, the excitement! Think of rubbing elbows with the BNFs! Of course, if all you can think of is rubbing elbows with female BNFs, you need plenty of instructions.

That's the purpose of this article. That, and a need to fill some space for which they couldn't sell advertising.

Anyhow, here are a few facts (damned few, to be exact) about conventions which I have gleaned from California, Canada, New Orleans and the bottom of an elevator shaft in Chicago's Hotel Morrison. I have put them in the form of a few simple (almost half-witted) rules and instructions which may benefit the neophyte conventioneer.

1. Upon arriving at the Hotel, go up to the desk and register under an obviously assumed name, such as P. H. Economou. Be very sure to get a room on the top floor. This is important. It means that when you look out the window

you won't be in danger of getting beaned by a bagful of hot water from above. Unless, of course, there's somebody on the roof. Come to think of it, there's always somebody on the roof. So why not register for accommodations on the roof? If somebody's up there, it might as well be you. Make sure you use at least 10-lb. bags. Water should be approximately 130° Fahrenheit. If you're not sure about the exact temperature, ask Willy Ley. He can tell as soon as the first bag hits him.

2. After you are comfortably settled in your room and have found out where all the necessities are located (that little dingus, for instance, that opens bottles on the wall) you can go down to the lobby and look for celebrities. If you're new at conventions, you might appreciate a few tips on how to identify the prominent guests. John W. Campbell, Jr., for example, is easily spotted. He has a Bonestell drawing on his beanie. The man with the exclusive, patented zap-gun is undoubtedly L. Sprague de Camp. The quiet, soft-spoken, almost inarticulate little fellow in the corner will turn out to be Sam Moskowitz. If you visit the bar, don't step on Forrest J Ackerman. Don't look for Bea Mahaffey or Evelyn Paige or Ginnie Saari or Lee Hoffman or any of the other gals, because chances are I will get there first and spirit them away. Go talk to Bob Tucker instead. Tell him you've found the Ten of Clubs and see how interested he gets.

3. Along about the second or third day of your stay, the convention will start. By this time, if you're any kind of a mixer at all, you'll be up in some room with a bunch from the Southern delegation.

These Southerners always welcome a mixer, to say nothing of ice. If you happen to meet them, your troubles are over. You can read about the convention later in some fanzine.

4. Let us suppose that you're a true faaaan and decide to actually *attend* convention sessions. The safest thing to do is get your *name* down on the program as a speaker or a performer.

Does the thought scare you? Don't worry! All you do is get your name down. Then, when you're scheduled to make an actual appearance, just send word you're ill, or can't make it, or weren't paroled in time. The Committee will find some poor goof to substitute for you, and you can sit back and have a good time.

5. You've bypassed all these obstacles and are actually going to the sessions. Well and good! Be sure you're amply supplied with soft drinks, reading matter, and the company of a few friends. You can enjoy yourself during the speeches if you have these diversions handy. Some seasoned fans like to bring their portable radios into the hall and listen to the ball game. But be courteous at all

times. Never turn the volume up too far. Remember, all around you are poor, tired fans who have had a hard night and want to sleep now.

6. If there's a Masquerade Ball, be sure to attend in correct civilian garb. Save your outlandish costumery for the regular sessions.

7. If you're a camera-fan, bring your camera and flashbulbs and make your presence felt. Whenever anyone gets up to speak, take his picture. Take a picture of the guy who introduces him. Take a picture of everybody listening to the speech. Take a picture of other people taking pictures of everybody listening to a guy making a speech. Take a picture of a guy taking a picture of a guy taking pictures of everybody listening to a guy making a speech. Go all out! Flash like crazy! Nobody will ever know that you actually don't have any *film* in the camera.

It's done at all the conventions; they apparently take picture after picture but nobody expects to see any when it's all over.

8. Keep your ears open! Remember, the main purpose of holding a convention is to collect and record every *faux pas* or personal remark made by fans and pros alike. These remarks, if in sufficiently bad taste, can be sold for big money to publishers of fanzines. If you don't get enough "quotes," sit down and invent a few that you think might be typical.

9. Above all, enjoy yourself! Take full advantage of the three fun-packed days and nights, the carefully-planned programs which have taken the convention committee many months of time, effort and anguish to prepare. Enter into this unique and amazing project to the utmost of your ability and get out of it all the pleasure you possibly can.

10. Then, go back home and prove yourself a true faaaan by grumbling that "It wasn't so hot" and "Jerry Bixby didn't play Ravel's *Piano Concerto for the Left Hand* as well as Casadesus" and "del Rey sounds like one of those editors to me."

Remember, unless you gripe, nobody will ever know you went to a convention!

Well, they're coming now to strap my arms again, so I'd better bring this to a close. If there's anything more you want to know about conventions, get hold of me at the next one.

I'll be there!

FROM A LETTER TO P. HOWARD LYONS

The word from Tucker is "First Fandom is NOT DEAD!"

And to prove it, Tucker himself swung into action last weekend, descending upon Chicago like a one-man horde of locusts. Accompanied by Fern (Tucker and Fern, what a bouquet they make together!) he issued a summons to all hands (and several feet) to take over the city in the name of First Fandom, or common indecency.

Lured by a spirit of morbid curiosity, I responded to his invitation and ventured into the purlieus as house-guest of Fritz Leiber.

On Wednesday evening, Tucker spoke to the University of Chicago Science Fiction Club. About 30 attendees heard him talk, and Fern and I applauded.

On Thursday, Tucker spoke to a class in sf writing at the YMCA. There's something for the memory-book — Tucker in a YMCA! Who said that never the twain shall meet? For that matter, the only reason I attended was because I'd been led to believe the meeting would be held in a YWCA.

Friday I moved into the Hotel Harrison, where Tucker and Fern had set up headquarters. Fern explained they'd left the baby home under a dishpan. Friday night we went out to the Dikty mansion for a party, where a fine time was had by brawl. The Dikty infant, little Sam, could not hold its liquor and passed out early.

On Saturday we three, augmented by Frank Robinson, Harriet Fellas and Earl Kemp, attended a Lollabrigida movie (Tucker is a great student of Italian cookery, and Gina is quite a dish) and a meeting of the Mystery Writers of America. This was followed by an old fashioned revival meeting at the Harrison Bar, during which several people had old fashioneds and had to be revived.

On Sunday we three (Tucker, Fern and I were by this time inseparable: at least, Fern and I were inseparable and Tucker was merely insufferable) walked over to the Field Museum to see an exhibit of Prehistoric Man. We spotted such outstanding types as *Homo Moskowitzus*, *Pithecanthropus Asimov* and *Early Neanderthal*, or *Acker Man*. Then on to Egyptology Room, where Tucker and I gazed reverently at the mummy of Impotentep.

Having cased the mummies, we hurried to view Jacques Tati in *Mr. Hulot's Holiday* — a film I very much wanted to see, and to which I dragged Tucker by claiming "Hulot" is really French for "Harlot." Thence to Ginny and Ollie Saari's home for the evening. They have a baby, a dog, two cats and lots of fun. On Monday the Tuckers went back to Bloomington and I returned to sanity.

It's hard, though, to get a clear picture of what Tucker is up to, besides his neck. He told some of the neo-fans at the University about the books he had written — *Slan*, and *The Demolished Man* and *The Lovers*. I never knew he'd done those titles under pseudonyms. The next night he told the YMCA class about ghostwriting editorials for somebody — I forget whether he said Campbell or Palmer: maybe it was both. At any rate, First Fandom is not dead. But after almost a week with Tucker, I damned near am.

PRO AND CON

Being a joint account of the recent affair at Bellefontaine, Ohio, by two people who didn't miss a single joint; namely and to wit:

JOE PRO and JOE FAN VIII

(Edited and expurgated, with considerable effort, by Robert Bloch.)

PRO: by Joe Pro

The fifth annual Midwescon was opened at Bellefontaine on May 22nd, although as usual, many of the gang got there a day or so earlier for the usual pre-conventional get-togethers.

In previous years, this highly informal gathering met at the resort out at Indian Lake, but this year the spot was not available. Apparently rumor had spread that Arthur C. Clarke might be expected and the good people of Indian Lake feared that the sight of Mr. Clarke prancing about in the diving mask, webs and fins he customarily wears might mislead the regular customers into thinking that they were periled by The Creature from the Black Lagoon.

Consequently the affair was held at the Hotel Ingalls, a local roach-ranch: although a number of foresighted pros took lodging in surrounding motels — feeling reasonably assured that fans could hardly drop bags of water out of the one-storey windows there. The fans and their bags were in evidence however: at least by outside report. Naturally, being a pro, I am unable to verify this at first hand, because I immediately took refuge in a schmoe-filled room and stayed there.

By Friday night nearly everyone had arrived. On Saturday I spotted such familiar figures as Philip José Farmer and Bette, Randall Garrett, Joe Gibson,

Evelyn Gold, Martin Greenberg, David Kyle, Lloyd Eshbach, E. E. Evans, Charles deVet and his wife, Wilson Tucker, Robert Bloch, Leigh Brackett, Edmond Hamilton, Ted Dikty and the fabulous Isaac Asimov.

It was a job squeezing them all into one room, but we managed. Saturday night there was some kind of film session, featuring pictures of the previous conventions, and I understand that this was very entertaining: unfortunately the cards were running against me and it was no time to break away.

Sunday noon was the occasion of the regular banquet, which I had hoped very much to attend: unfortunately the cards were working for me, and it was no time to break away.

Sunday night many of us joined Doc Barrett and Mrs. Barrett at dinner, and later met out at a motel on the road where Tucker had a room, as did the Smiths. Canadians were also installed there, including a Mr. Mallard, Mr. Grantz or Granch, and a couple named McLoon, or Bolton . . . some such name. They were very boring and insisted on talking about sf, much to our disgust.

By Monday it was all over, and the various die-hard attendees drifted off to all points of the compass. The convention itself was more of an ambulatory, peripatetic bull-session than anything else: the hotel was a bit too small to contain roughly 200 people, and as a result it was impossible for everyone to remain under one roof at the same time. For this reason there were fewer parties and less congregating in a single spot. As usual, the pros were their sweet, quiet little selves, and only the fans made any disturbance. Ever since Willis came to America, these creatures show a tendency to become too big for their britches. The next thing you know, they'll want to be playing poker themselves! But, aside from the fans, the convention was a most enjoyable affair.

CON: by Joe Fan VIII

The first fifth was opened at the Midwescon shortly after I arrived, a day or so ahead of the pro "gang" . . . in order to avoid their usual unconventional get-togethers.

In previous years this mob met at Indian Lake, but since last year's disgraceful episode of Arthur C. Clarke and the waterpistol, it was necessary to move into town. Clarke did not show up this year, and it was gratifying to see that a number of other pros were missing: owing to the sf market slump, I suppose some of them find it difficult to raise enough money to get out on bail, and in time we may see the last of them at conventions such as these, speed the blessed day.

As a result the convention took place at the Hotel Ingalls, a fine hotel with paper-thin walls and unusually large keyholes: the halls gave off fine echoes whenever a firecracker exploded, and before 24 hours had passed, enough bags of water were dropped out of the windows to make you think the hotel was located in Venice. I understand the town itself is quite nice: being a fan of course I wouldn't know, because I never left the hotel: just holed up and made myself comfortable in a bloke-filled room and stayed there.

Most everybody got there Friday night: I saw Harlan Ellison and Ted Wagner, Earl and Nancy Kemp, Jim Harmon, Ian MacCauley, Norm Browne, Don Ford, Stan Skirvan, Lou Tabakow, Harriet Fellas, Hal and Nancy Shapiro, Rita Krohne, Phyllis Economou from Florida, McKeown, Grant, Millard, etc. Somebody said Asimov was there too (whoever he is).

Of course, most of the fans got together in one room (whose it was I never did find out) and Saturday night there was some kind of movie program, featuring Laurel and Hardy and Chaplin comedies. I meant to go there, but we were getting out a convention one-shot and I couldn't leave.

Sunday noon was banquet time, and again I tried to make it, but the mimeo wasn't working and I was covered with ink, so I passed it up.

Sunday night a lot of us stayed at the hotel and gabbed around: commenting on several of the unusual figures that had showed up. Two of them are rumored to be pr-gn-nt, and this only confirms the stories you hear about pros. A couple of the latter drifted into the hotel, but they were very boring and insisted on talking about parties and good times, much to our disgust.

By Monday it was all over, the last firecracker was shot, and we dispersed. It had been very hard to sperse in the first place, because the hotel was small and it was impossible for everyone to remain under one bed at the same time. For this reason there were more parties and as usual, the fans were their modest, shy selves, while only the pros made any disturbance. Ever since Willis came to America and began fawning on pros, they've gotten too big for their hats. But aside from them, the convention was fine.

AT THE HEADWATERS

On Tuesday before the Cleveland convention, Dean and Jean Grennell drove up here with Bob and Barbara Silverberg in tow. They had planed in from Darkest Brooklyn and were staying at the Fond du Lac Children's Center as Dean's guests, prior to attending the convention. Acting on the theory that the best way to learn how to survive underwater is to practice in the bathtub first, *à la* Houdini, Grennell decided they should be exposed to my company for an evening. So up they came, and we indulged in a few tentative obscenities during the coarse of the evening. Bob and Barbara impressed me as very nice people and in my heart of hearts I pitied them for what they were about to encounter in Cleveland. I spent part of the evening warning young Barbara about Tucker, and demonstrated some of the holds.

On Thursday I flew to Cleveland and goshwowboyoboy. There isn't much point going into detail: I guess I'm queer for conventions because I always have so much fun. Wilson Tucker, boy octogenarian, was on hand with Fern and David. Tucker has trained his child well: during poker games he holds David on his lap and the kid palms the aces. As soon as the child gets a few more teeth he will make a nice bottle-opener, too.

I also encountered Shirley Hoffman. We celebrated our reunion with a breakfast in a kosher delicatessen and drank toasts to Jefferson Davis, Alexander Stephens, Stonewall Jackson, Robert E. Lee, Beauregard, Longstreet, Mosby, Cantrell, Quantrill, Judah P. Benjamin, Rhett Butler and Kissin' Jim Folsom . . . all Big Name Fans of yesteryear. Lee looks mighty good, but then she is mighty good, and I was right pleased to see her sashaying around again.

As to the convention itself what can I say? Everybody and his brother was there, but I kept looking for his sister. On Tuesday the little men came around with the Flit-guns and I went home.

But not alone. A little band of hardy pioneers gathered at the headwaters of Independence, Missouri, in the tiny haberdashery store of Harry S Truman and pledged mutual assistance in the westward trek across the plains. Vowing an early start, we pushed off at noon into the wilds of darkest Ohio, surrounded by hordes of howling Cleveland Indians.

The party consisted of Wilson Tucker, grizzled old mountain-man, his Squaw Fern, and David, his get . . . plus Canuck William D. Grant (no relation to Damnyankee Grant the Butcher) and his mother. There was also a Pekingese, by far the best-behaved of the entire party in that it neither spoke nor wet. Nothing came out of either end during the entire trip, which is more than you can say for the rest of us.

We drove steadily until about 10 P.M. and then unsteadily until about 4 A.M., at which time we arrived in Ludington, Michigan. Now it was my plan to drive right on into Wisconsin, but upon arriving at Ludington I was thwarted by the appearance of a large body of water. This turned out to be Lake Michigan, which I swear wasn't on my map at all. Anyway, after hasty consultation, we came up with two plans: (1) To take the ferry across and (2) to build a raft.

Unfortunately, Fern refused pointblank to build the raft. So we took the ferry. We arrived in Weyauwega, and a deplorable condition, the following afternoon. Marion, who happens to be my wife (I keep telling her not to feel bad, it could happen to anyone) greeted us with the opener, and the second stage of the convention began. It lasted from Wednesday to Saturday. On Thursday night Dean and Jean arrived. On Friday, Marty Greenberg came up — he'd driven around, via Chicago. We showed films of past conventions and lived a little.

Saturday I went down to Milwaukee for the TV show and the body was shipped home the following day.

It was a nice do.

A LETTER TO A CONVENTION-GOER

Dear Wreck:

Maybe that isn't your name now — but that's what you'll be after four days at an sf convention. I know. I attended my first one back in 1946, and since then my friends tell me I've aged a good ten years.

That is, my friends *would* tell me — if I had any friends left.

Unfortunately, when you sit down at a poker table, friendship is left behind. And when you get up again, everything else is left behind, too. If you've ever wondered why it is that so many professional writers spend all year pounding out stories, the answer is simple — they're just trying to pay off their poker debts to Bob Tucker.

But I forget. Some of you readers are doubtless new to these sf conventions. You probably don't even know who Bob Tucker is. Well, I can tell you. He's the guy you shouldn't play poker with.

Of course, sf conventions aren't just one long poker game. One of their attractions lies in the fact that they offer something for just about everybody. People with a serious interest in scientific studies, such as chemistry, can always stand at the bar and watch how drinks are mixed.

People interested in sheer horror can wait around for the next day, and the inquests.

Then too, there's usually a program. This is the most healthy aspect of an sf convention. People who have suffered from insomnia for years tell me they get immediate relief the moment a speaker opens his mouth.

On the other hand, those who stay awake and actually listen to the speakers tell me afterwards they just can't fall asleep. Afraid of nightmares, I suppose.

After all, who would want to meet Isaac Asimov in a dream? (Let's face it: who would want to meet Isaac Asimov, period?)

Incidentally, this brings up an interesting point about convention manners. There's this curious custom of insults. Now I have already, in the course of this little message, managed to insult both Bob Tucker and Isaac Asimov. I do so merely as a matter of form — it's the usual thing to make snide remarks about the people you like.

Actually, Tucker and Asimov are two of the nicest people I've ever met: and I've met plenty in my time — folks like Dillinger, Jack the Ripper and E. E. Smith, Ph.D.

If this is your first sf convention, there are a few tips you may be interested in — particularly, if you happen to be a bellboy.

To begin with, eat all your meals in your room. This business of finding a friend and making a date to meet for dinner at 6 o'clock sharp just never seems to work out. Because your friend tells another friend and he tells another. You end up waiting around until 9:30 and finally eat your meal with 48 people and Forrest J Ackerman.

Another thing: don't waste your time trying to find your favorite author. I remember, in Chicago, how desperately anxious I was to meet Harlan Ellison. Somebody said he was in the bar lounge. Well, I went down there and I looked under 65 different tables and never located him. Of course, I *did* manage to meet 65 *other* authors that way.

One of them even turned out to be myself.

Then there's the matter of pretty girls. If you happen to be a pretty girl yourself, you probably won't be interested in meeting any — in any event, you won't have time, because you'll have your hands full with Dave Kyle. But if you're not a pretty girl, chances are you'll want to find one.

Sooner or later you'll probably see a big crowd gathered around somebody in the lobby or in the convention suite. Lots of wolfish-looking fan types, milling around someone in the center.

Well, take my advice and don't go near them. They haven't got a pretty girl at all. They're just talking to some nobody like John W. Campbell, Jr.

One of the interesting things about this particular convention is the Masquerade Ball. Every convention has held a Masquerade Ball, in which people turn up with outlandish costumes, green faces, etc. But usually the affair is held on the last night. This time the Masquerade Ball is planned for the first evening. Which means for once that most of the green faces will be the result of makeup.

But conventions have their serious side, too. For seventeen years, sf fans and pros have perpetuated the custom of getting together for fun, friendship and fraternity. Except for a lapse during World War II, these have been annual affairs. Thousands of people have travelled hundreds of thousands of miles to attend. I speak collectively, of course. But a convention such as this *is* a collective entity: a collection of representative humanity interested in a common hobby.

As such, I find it interesting. Labor Day weekend is a traditional time of relaxation . . . a time when millions of earnest souls sit watching nine men try to bat a ball better than nine other men . . . a time when carefree competitive spirits sally forth on the public highways, eager to set a new record for traffic deaths and destruction.

Maybe I'm foolish for not joining in. Maybe I'm foolish to spend *my* Labor Day weekends at sf conventions, which are like nothing on Earth.

Still, you know how I feel about Earth. It's a nice place to visit, but I wouldn't want to live there.

Thoughtfully,
Robert Bloch

SURROGATE IN '58

If you see anything dirty here it's probably my neck sticking out. Writing this in the later part of July, I have no assurance that Los Angeles will capture the World Science Fiction Convention in 1958 — hence, out comes my neck. You might say I am sticking my neck out on the end of a limb, but if you do you'd better go back and have another look at an anatomy text.

And while you're doing so (and probably sneaking a peek at those fascinating color plates of the pelvis) the rest of us will carry on and discuss plans and possibilities for the 1958 convention.

I'm not quite sure in my own mind (or anyone else's, for that matter) under just what circumstances Rick Sneary originated the Slogan, "South Gate in '58." The whole episode seems somewhat cloudy — or, as California citizens might say, smoggy.

For many years this fannish cry had little or no relevancy; it was in a class with derogatory remarks concerning Yngvi or inquiries concerning the damaging of a certain Mr. Courtney's property. Fan-historians succeeded in tracing the Yngvi quotation back to its source, and I myself hereby claim credit for running down the Courtney item.

Just for the record, I'm going to set that little matter straight once and for all before proceeding. Many people seem to think that the query "Who sawed Courtney's boat?" originated in an *Esquire* article. Not so. The source is much, much older, and I spent many years tracing it. Finally I ran across the *original* quotation in — of all places — the Bible. Where, of course, it reads: "Who sawed Noah's Ark?"

But I'm pretty sure that you won't find "South Gate in '58" in the Bible; unless it appears in the form of a disguised prophecy in *Revelations* along with that stuff about the end of the world and the coming of the Great Beast.

Until the matter is settled by a higher authority, such as T. M. Carr or William Rotsler, we'll have to assume that Sneary is responsible. All through the late 'Forties and early 'Fifties the fannish chant went on: "South Gate in '58!"

And now, of course, retribution is at hand. Chickens come home to rooster. So, chances are there *will* be a Los Angeles convention next year — if not in South Gate, at least within the general area. The damage has been done. And the next question is: "Who'll clean up the mess?"

Mr. Sneary and some of his cohorts have already taken certain steps: the spring FAPA mailing included an elaborate questionnaire concerning just what prospective attendees might want in the way of a convention program. Unfortunately, I'm afraid the questions are phrased so that answers will not be very helpful. It is all right for Sneary and Company to inquire "Do you want a banquet?" and "How do you feel about movies?" but when they follow it up, as they did, with "What do you think about balls?" the only possible answer is: "I wouldn't be without them." No, it would appear that the Planning Committee will be needing some help and a few suggestions. My first suggestion, as an old hand at this sort of affair, is "change your name and go into hiding until 1959." If this one is ruled out — and I've a hunch it will be — then it's up to us to find a practical solution to this convention problem.

We all know that conventions have become big affairs and difficult to manage. In contemplating the prospects for '58 it's easy to envision a situation where a thousand or more people pour into Los Angeles and repeat the spectacle of recent years.

This means that the poor convention committee will have to scour the town looking for a big hotel that has no airconditioning in its halls; one which will cooperate by running just a single elevator, with an operator skilled at catching passengers' heads in the door; one which will guarantee to set aside a bloc of rooms at $7 per day until the convention actually opens, whereupon prices will be boosted to $12 and attendees' rooms scattered all over the place for the convenience of the house detective.

This takes time and effort. Wasted time and needless effort, it seems to me. I've been trying to think of solutions. Holding the convention in the Los Angeles sewers would probably eliminate the need of securing a spot minus airconditioning; on the other hand, acoustics are such as to render such a location inadvisable. Those of us who have heard Moskowitz sound forth in an ordinary room must tremble in dread at the prospect of having that voice magnified in the natural echo-chamber of a sewer. Besides, the sewer location would probably make the whole convention the target of a running gag.

Finding the hotel with 1,000 rooms and just one working elevator isn't easy, either. My alternative suggestion — just take any hotel and merely *remove* the elevators, leaving nothing but empty shafts — meets with objections from the union. Granted that it's much easier to slip down an elevator shaft and get to your destination in a hurry than to wait for the coming of an empty car, the business appears impractical.

Then there's always the banquet. Usually the hotel provides its own staff facilities for this but in the event they can't meet the lower standards of the usual convention meal, it might be possible to get in an outside catering service, such as a local tannery.

But why bother? Why, when there's a perfectly natural solution to the entire question: merely turn back the clock to 1946 and carry on with the Los Angeles convention of that year. We oldtimers who attended this primitive tribal ritual can well remember just how simple it was. The convention itself was held in an abandoned chicken-coop across the street from MacArthur Park. I don't recall who furnished the entertainment for the program but I think it was a mortician. There was no problem about handling the affair: everything was turned over to Forrest J Ackerman, who merely passed out the first day and never returned to the scene of the crime. The banquet menu was simple and typically Californian — Nutburgers, Squidburgers, Spiderburgers and things like that.

By limiting the attendance to the original 150 or 200 who showed up in '46, the committee would avoid most of their worst difficulties, including Anthony Boucher and other upstarts who have since polluted fandom with their fancy notions, their use of correct English, and other concepts which have robbed us of our Sense of Wonder. Make no mistake about it, that Sense of Wonder was *the* big feature of the 1946 convention. We were always wondering just what in hell would happen next.

For example, there was the matter of the film showing. I believe that *Metropolis* was originally scheduled, or *The Shape of Things To Come* — whichever Ackerman got the biggest rake-off on. So nobody was really surprised when the movie turned out to be *One Million BC*. (That "BC" means "Before Cinemascope," naturally.) Those who objected to the scanty banquet fare were thus compensated by being presented with this turkey. The opus starred Victor Mature way back in the days when he was young and known as Victor Immature. It was a real educational treat, revealing such little-realized bits as the fact that prehistoric cave women wore lipstick and put on uplift bras before zipping up their leopard-skins.

Unfortunately, just as the film was beginning to get interesting — in fact, when it appeared that in this one scene the heroine had forgotten to pull up her zipper — something went haywire with the projector, or the projectionist. I forgot which, and so does the projectionist, a Mr. Tucker. As a result, the showing was never completed.

I submit therefore that the 1958 convention return to the 1946 program and merely re-run *One Million BC* again. Ackerman can collapse once more, Burbee can climax the whole affair by telling the Watermelon Story (since filmed as *The Bad Seed*) and what more do you want?

If, however, you *do* insist on more — and I'm afraid the committee and some of the guests may do just that — then I've one final proposal.

That, of course, is my "Surrogate in '58" plan. Under this proposition, there is no convention hall, no banquet, no entertainment, no speakers, and not even a convention committee. In fact, there's not even a convention.

Everybody merely stays home from the middle of August to the middle of September or thereabouts. You take about four days off during that time and lock yourself in a hot, airtight room, put on a continuous tape-recording of Mossolov's *Steel Foundry,* gulp down a fifth of Jim Beam every three hours and a bottle of aspirin each night, and stay awake during the entire period. At the end of the week you emerge, feeling exactly as you would if you'd attended a convention.

Then, with the money you saved, you can all go off to the *next* affair . . . which I plan to promote with the slogan: "Hollywood & Vine in '59!"

THE INCREDIBLE HEAD-SHRINKING MAN

From time to time I have taken poison-pen in hand and scrawled a few venomous comments upon the activities of those who make our sf movies. I have suggested that these merchants of *papier mâché* menace, these apostles of mad science, these manufacturers of monstrosities, have done a disservice to the sf field by packaging their nonsense under the sf label.

It is only fair, however, to consider their side of the matter. I do not refer to the common argument that their efforts are justified because they are in business to make money — the same rationalization applies to narcotics peddlers and the purveyors of eight-page cartoon booklets.

No, the producers of sf films have another, and much more potent defense for their products.

They are practical psychologists; they are the incredible head-shrinking men referred to in the title of this memorandum. They are the people who provide harmless outlets for paranoids; who gratify the wish-fulfillments of all those who feel a need to rebel against authority.

It is easy to see that those of us who are conscious that we are living in "A World I Never Made" can take a certain degree of satisfaction in seeing a pictorial fantasy depicting the invasion, disruption or even partial destruction of such a world. Hence the popularity of the so-called sf movies in which the cities are razed and the Earth is menaced. It is equally easy to understand why less aggressive fantasies involving mere escape from intolerable conditions are gratified by movies of flight to other planets. Thematically, such movies supply a need.

Less immediately obvious, but still discernible, are the Authority-defying elements which form the basis of many of the standard sf movie plots.

We live in a world dominated by Authority; blue-coated, khaki-clad, white-robed and armed with title and degree. Hence it is no accident (and a cause for inward gloating rather than concern on the part of audiences) when the standard sf plot shows us a picture of the Dumb Sheriff, the Stupid Cop, the Baffled Big Brass, the Smugly Ignorant Doctor and the Half-Witted Professor.

In an era where every medium (including the motion picture screen, in the majority of realistic pictures) steadily glorifies the Law, the Military, the Medical Profession and the Scientist, the sf film offers almost the sole outlet for rebellion-fantasies. Here is the policeman who is too brainless to believe the story about the Purple Cows from Mars, even when this smart little freckle-faced kid brings him proof in the form of a Purple Cowpatch. Here is a high-ranking army officer who can't stop the Armless Women of Venus from their ravagings, no matter how loudly he bawls commands. Here is a doctor who can't cure the mysterious disease which trails in the wake of the invaders from the fabulous planet of Gonnorhea. And here is the scientist, helpless to combat the Giant Intestinal Worms.

There is a large audience which takes pleasure in such spectacles and let us not forget it. The success of the sf movie-makers lies in the very fact that *they* haven't.

Not only do many of these pictures portray Authorities as incompetent or even idiotic; often they gratify the public with a presentation of the Authority as Evil. In every film where the monsters take over human beings, it's axiomatic that they either usurp the bodies of law-enforcement officers or enlist their active aid as allies. Hence the sf film again successfully violates one of the standard taboos and offers us a steady succession of Wicked Police Chiefs, Mad Doctors and Cracked Eggheads. Much to the delight of every child and every childish adult. How frequently, in these same films, do we encounter the undisguised situation where Parents become the corrupted agents of the "aliens" and the innocent Kiddies are menaced? Here is one of the most common fantasies of rebellion offered nakedly and openly as entertainment.

Fantasies involving dislocation of bodies, changes in size and relationship, etc., are often encountered by the psychiatrist. He can now, thanks to sf movies, encounter them on the wide screen in such offerings as *The Incredible Shrinking Man*, where inferiority-feelings, the hatred of spiders and cats, the unconscious masculine protest of the small boy against the Gigantic Mother are effectively presented to evoke full response. It is possible for any psychotherapist to have himself a large ball by merely winnowing the symbolism which runs rampant through this and many similar films.

Whether such dramatized fantasies of protest effectively drain off the aggressive feelings of the afflicted or merely intensify their tensions is not for the layman to say. Let the Dr. Werthams of this world make a big buck by presenting their opinions in the women's magazines.

But the next time you visit your neighboring cinema to witness a new sf epic, take note of the company releasing it; then wonder to yourself whether or not the producer's name should rightfully be replaced by the legend, PARANOID PICTURES PRESENTS.

PETE KELLY'S BLUE DRAGNET

I was a bit disappointed, figuring that you medium-fi, warm-rod, refrigerated-jazz addicts in Canada would have discovered and commented upon a film entitled *Pete Kelly's Blues.* Apparently, however, it has not played Toronto, so as we used to say down at the fertilizer plant, a few words are in ordure.

Pete Kelly's Blues is a typical specknicolor techtacle, starring the drag of *Dragnet*, Jack Webb.

Jack Webb fascinates me. Those of you who know of my passion for oldtime movie actor Buster Keaton can easily understand why. Jack Webb is a frozen-faced performer alongside of whom Ed Sullivan appears to be another Orson Welles. Webb's histrionic repertoire consists of exactly two expressions. He looks like (a) a man who has a fear of sitting down in something wet, or (b) a man who *has* sat down in something wet and isn't sure if he's responsible or not. But in neither case does he want anyone else to suspect. I have not seen anyone quite like Jack Webb since 1932, in a picture called *White Zombie.*

Mr. Webb undertakes (and I use the term advisedly) the role of one Pete Kelly, a jazz musician who purportedly flourished in Kansas City, circa 1923-28. His small combo is employed at a restaurant-speakeasy, and it is easy to see that here is a real bunch of Dedicated Cats. They Worship The Ground He Walks On, and every night they Play Their Hearts Out. Kelly plays frequent horn solos and addresses the instrument like an orangutan trying to swallow a banana. There is a vague atmosphere of latent homosexuality about this bunch as depicted; Mr. Kelly is forever brushing off the attentions of a wealthy, feather-brained and feather-cut blonde chick who pursues him with all the passionate abandon of Harlan Ellison wooing a potential subscriber to *Dimen-*

sions. Mr. Kelly will have none of that, even though said chick is none other than Mrs. Bernard Schwartz in person. In Mr. Kelly's defence it must be said that the chick is dressed distastefully in exaggerated 1925 style-parodies and is depicted initially as a cretinous type. However, once she invades his bedroom and discovers that he owns a budgerigar, she is not to be put off.

Meanwhile, the band is taken over by a mobster (well-played by Edmund O'Brien) who is being pursued by a detective (well-played by Andy Devine) and who foists off onto the band his chirp inamorata (well-played by Peggy Lee). The mobster kills one of Kelly's boys, beats up and schizophrenicates the chirp, extorts from the band and finally Mr. Kelly decides that Something Must Be Done About This because it apparently is going to reach a point where such antics will affect his music and interfere with the beat. So there is a bang-up shooting-type finale in a deserted ballroom, a chandelier comes down in a Hitchcockian way and the villain and his henchmen get it in the end.

So much (and too much) for the plot. I happen to like the performances of the three thespians enumerated above, and much of the music has its own special nostalgia for one who can remember the *Hit Parade of 1926*, etc. But what bothers me about the film, aside from Jack Webb and the cliché plot, is the treatment of both the jazz and the period. In recent years it has suddenly become *de rigueur* to present the Twenties in the satirical light as the Gay Nineties. Sparked by Broadway musicals like *Gentlemen Prefer Blondes, The Boy Friend,* etc., everyone has jumped into the act with both feet. TV "Spectaculars" in particular dote on copying the obvious burlesque elements, and as a result the Twenties have become a mélange of raccoon coats, ukeleles, hip-flasks, Charleston dancers and Wild Parties — all merely as an excuse to have a lot of chorus girls shag around in a Big Production Number. And the music has suffered the same treatment. If Pete Kelly's boys are supposed to typify the jazz musicians of the Good Old Days, then I must have been living in another dimension at the time instead of in Chicago.

All of which may seem very much beside the point to you people until you stop to reflect that unless geriatrics perform some major miracle, some day you'll be almost as old as I am now — and in turn looking back twenty or twenty-five years to a period which will then be known as the Fabulous Fifties. And you will feel a certain uneasiness, then, I'm sure, if you happen to see that decade depicted as an era in which everyone owned a sports car, worshiped at the shrines of Brubeck, Mulligan or Kenton, spent all their waking hours watching TV and seemed to have no personal identity aside from that. Most of all you will be inclined to resent the implication that the young people of the Fifties were complete and utter goofs with absolutely nothing under their crewcuts or dovetails; the astute writer or producer who characterizes them will make certain that they speak only in the be-bop lingo of 1953 or thereabouts. And this will be accepted as "the way things were" by the current viewers; a gay, romantic and carefree period When You And I Were Young, Muggsy.

It is such blatant fakery which I must deplore; particularly when I reflect on the opportunities they had to make a really fine, honest picture about Jazz in the Twenties. What they came up with was a hunk of unabashed hokum, and my lunch.

THE EALING ART

There was a time when I could take a snobbish sort of pride in the fact that I seemed to know considerably more about English cinema, for example, than many of my friends. I admit there were occasions when I delighted in pulling my J. Arthur Rank on them with references to Ernest Thesiger, Tom Walls, Jack Buchanan and others who cavorted across strips of British celluloid back in the Thirties.

Those were the poverty-stricken days of the Depression; for some time it was possible to give credence to the claim that the greasy, half-naked gentleman who struck a gong at the beginning of a J. Arthur Rank production was J. Arthur Rank himself. Over here in the States, we used to get English movies as the second feature in double-bills, but surprisingly few people seemed to stick around and see them.

As one of the few, it was my privilege to make the simultaneous acquaintance of Alfred Hitchcock and Peter Lorre way back in 1934 in *The Man Who Knew Too Much*: to see American actors such as Edward Everett Horton in such odd but enthralling efforts as *The Man in the Mirror*: to admire Roland Young and Lillian Gish in *Buried Alive* and to familiarize myself with the work of such teams as Basil Radford and Naunton Wayne.

As late as 1951 I could enjoy an occasional evening with an expatriate like Milwaukee television director Ivor McLaren — who had worked in films and musical comedy for years in England — cutting up old bits about Cicely Courtneidge, Wilfred Hyde-White, Olive Sloane and a host of others; much to his amazement and to the bafflement of the Yankees.

But these days, alas, are gone forever. Television has reared its ugly tube. Today the American TV viewer is inundated with imports. In our particular area I venture to say we receive as many British films as local products, and Naunton Wayne has become almost as familiar as John.

Googie Withers, Dennis Price, John Mills, Aubrey Mather, Sonia Dresdel, Derek Farr — we get them all. And of course Guinness and Hitchcock and Sir Cedric Hardnose are household names in America today.

So my day of glory as an expert in obscurantism is long since past. I shall be forced to study up on Kabuchi dancers or Grand Guignol performers of the Twenties if I want to maintain my status as a wisenheimer or wise boy of the Beaux Arts.

But it is interesting to see this cavalcade of British cinema rushing past on millions of television screens over here — particularly if one holds to the belief (as I do) that the movies of a nation unconsciously reflect a good deal of its *mores* and attitudes.

The subtle differences in characterization, for example, afford clues which emphasize the difference in British and American temperament.

English heroes, for instance, are usually much less self-consciously attitudinizing than American ones. Outside of farce comedies such as the Bob Hope films, American movies seldom permit the presence of a hero who declares himself to be afraid of anything. Once in a great while we get a cautious hero (such as Gary Cooper in *High Noon*) and this switch seems to greatly impress and almost shock our audiences. Whereas English films are full of unwilling heroes. The British scientists of *School for Secrets*, for example, would never be permitted on our screens unless shown in terms of broad comedy. Come to think of it, Ralph Richardson would never be cast in anything vaguely resembling the semi-heroic role he played here, to say nothing of being handed outright leads such as his *Murder on Monday* or *The Fallen Idol*. He's much too old.

Yes, we have plenty of ageing heroes ourselves (Cooper, Gable, Grant, Cotten, Stewart) but they make every attempt to appear youthful and athletic and sexy as all get-out. Once in a while some of them, notably Stewart and Cooper, are even allowed to get just a wee bit tired — but show them a villain with a gun or a knife or a girl with an oversized bust and at once they rise to the challenge.

The sex-situation, by the way, offers striking contrasts. British films, generally speaking, are both more forthright and more matter-of-fact about sex-relationships. Dinah Sheridan, in *Genevieve*, sprawls on the bed and tells her husband, "make love to me." In an American film she would leer, wriggle, cling, partially disrobe — but keep her mouth shut. We are often visually explicit, but seldom verbally direct.

As to the matter-of-fact part: in British films a happy marital or pre-marital or extra-marital relationship is subtly implied by a mere showing of a harmonious relationship between the couples in question. There is seldom any overt display of affection. In American films the formula is different; there must be constant muzzlings and clinches to "get across" the idea that Daddy and Mama are still That Way About Each Other even if they have kiddies, or that young Miss Masochist still gets a wallop out of young Mr. Sadist.

The first time I heard the word "hell" used in its common profane connotation on the screen was in *Twenty Thousand Horsemen*: since that time I've noted that "hell" and "damn" are common expressions in English offerings — but it has only been in the past two years that one finds such language in American movies. Even so recent a picture as *The Blackboard Jungle* evoked a gasp from the typical audience when a knife-wielding juvenile delinquent told his teacher to "go to hell." Get that, now — nobody was shocked because the kid pulled a knife on his teacher. What shocked them was the fact that he came right out and said a nasty word on the screen. Bloody strange, what?

In terms of plot and treatment, differences are so great that they have been generally noted by critics. Few American producing units would essay a *Black Lace* or a *Rocking Horse Winner* — few would tackle a film like *The Third Man* and risk an ending where Joseph Gotten and Valli forego a clinch. The impudent and inspired conclusion of *The Captain's Paradise* might or might not get by — certainly we'd never permit the implication that the Captain was not legally (although bigamously) united with Yvonne de Carlo unless he Paid The Penalty.

It has often been said that British films are more "talky" than American; that they are more "episodic"; that they have a slower pace.

If so, I regard these circumstances as blessings in that the very plethora of dialogue and wealth of casual asides and incidents affords us viewers over here with a partial insight into seemingly realistic evidence of the national characteristics.

American minor and bit roles are usually assigned to "stock types" — over and over again one sees the same clerks, flunkeys, second-assistant hoodlums, yokels, western bar-room habitues, policemen, etc. Often the same people play the same roles in endless repetition. And almost always, they repeat the same dialogue. Lord pity the English if they attempt to learn anything about American attitudes and ways from the few pitiful stereotypes generally handed out in our films! I have the feeling there's far more naturalism, far more realism, afforded in the average British cinema effort.

Of course I have yet to run into a counterpart of a John Berry or a George Charters in an English movie — but I suppose you have *your* censorship to consider over there, too.

Meanwhile, rest assured that motion pictures, in their own way, serve to cement the bonds of American and British fandom. Any day now I look forward to seeing Robert Morley and Cecil Parker indulging in a rousing session of Ghoodminton while, in the background, Dame Edith Evans whips up a spot of tea.

THE PAST RECAPTURED

or, Down Memory Lane With Butterfly Net and Restraint-Jacket

Ever so often, while attending an sf convention, I am approached by a teenage neofan.

If the neofan happens to be female, I immediately demand to inspect her birth certificate before allowing our acquaintance to ripen.

If (as is usually the disappointing case) the fan is male, we generally exchange a few words; and usually to my profit, since I've picked up a lot of dirty words that way.

But if we talk for any length of time, sooner or later the neofan gets around to asking the fatal question: "Tell me, Dad — what was it like to be a fan 'way back in the early days?"

By "the early days" he's usually talking about the 1931-35 period, known to us historians as the Dark Ages. What kind of a world was it?

Jayne Mansfield hadn't been born, nor Anita Ekberg whelped. Marilyn Monroe was still *virgo intacta*, according to many of her biographers. Gertrude M. Carr was not yet a grandmother; presumably she was revelling in the administration of Herbert Hoover and preparing to go underground as Franklin Delano Roosevelt assumed office in March of '33.

Can you imagine what it was like to live in a world where Elvis Presley didn't even *exist*? Talk about a sense of wonder — we had it! It was a world in which the Model T still roamed the streets in plenitude. There were horse-troughs too, although these were fast disappearing along with such other primitive manifestations as organ grinders, junk wagons, derby hats, arm-bands, detachable collars, wind-up phonographs, Irish Mails for the kiddies and headphones on radio sets. Radio sets (again, for the benefit of you late-comers) are pretty hard to describe. The nearest I can come to it is to ask you to imagine a TV set with a broken picture tube. Like ours, after Elvis appears.

Perhaps you can manage to visualize this — but can you visualize an entire universe operating full blast without the presence of Lee Hoffman, Harlan Ellison, Peter Vorzimer, Bob Silverberg, Jim Harmon, Gregg Calkins or Peter Graham? A world in which Sam Moskowitz was still speaking with a soprano voice?

If you can, don't bother to read any farther. Just set your visualization down in book form and call it *Utopia*.

Actually, I'm only kidding. One of the greatest defects of fandom and fanning in the Thirties was the lack of just such an assortment as the above-named. Anyone who has ever read *The Immortal Storm* will realize that early fandom was pretty much of a paper-airplane proposition: flimsily constructed and incapable of soaring to any height.

It wasn't until midway in the decade that fans actually began to organize into clubs holding regular meetings — and then, only in a few major metropolitan areas. The great preoccupation of the time was not with writing or communication but with reading and collecting; the social aspect was dominated by politics and feuding. The era of fannish friendship seems to have come later, when conventions began and fans started visiting one another.

When I entered fandom, the Great Depression raged; it was the time of the Lindbergh Kidnapping, of Prohibition and Rudy Vallee and other evils; of Bobby Jones and Technocracy and Bank Nite at the movies.

I got in through the back door, as a fan correspondent of H. P. Lovecraft and the Lovecraft Circle . . . but although pieces of mine saw print as early as 1934 in Crawford's *Marvel Tales* and Hornig's *Fantasy Fan*, I met more pros than fans. The only fan I *did* meet, prior to 1937, was the fabulous Jack Darrow, who dropped in for a visit one Sunday afternoon in Milwaukee. Darrow vied in those days for the dubious distinction of "Number One Fan" and I felt properly humble in his presence. He name-dropped all over the place, as I well recall, because after he left I had to sweep up all those names from off the living room rug.

So, while I gradually got personally acquainted with Stanley Weinbaum, Ray Palmer, Ralph Milne Farley, Farnsworth Wright, Otto Binder, August Derleth, Donald Wandrei, Julius Schwartz, Mort Weisinger and Otis Adelbert Kline — all of whom I met in either Milwaukee or Chicago in the mid-Thirties — I knew nothing of fandom.

That's because, aside from a few fanzines, there was little way in which I could get acquainted with the field. If any APAs existed, they were APAthetic. It wasn't until 1937 when I went to California to visit Henry Kuttner that I learned more about the fan field, at first hand. On that visit I met C.L. Moore, Fritz Leiber and Bob Olsen — but I also had my baptism of fire my first visit to a fan club.

It was, of course, the LASFS, and there I became acquainted with such long-ago and far-away figures as Fred Shroyer, Russ Hodgkins, Jim Mooney, Morojo and some pesty teenage kid name of Bradbury. The meeting was presided over by a Mr. Ackerman, who has since won some fame as a movie reviewer.

In 1939 I visited New York, but met only pros. Nobody so much as invited me to a Hydra Club orgy.

News of the first convention failed to stir me. The second affair, held in nearby Chicago, tempted me a bit — but I hardly felt I could afford the fifteen or twenty bucks for a weekend.

So during that far off decade, I went my proud and lonely way . . . reading and writing for the prozines . . . turning out bits and pieces for such fannish efforts as *Unusual Stories* (believe me, they were!) and *Fantasy and Science Fantasy Correspondent*; a crudzine to end all crudzines called *The Phantagraph*, which was edited at various times by a certain Wollheim and a certain Kyle.

Looking back on those early years, I can detect only one glimmer of consolation. As yet, I had never run into Bob Tucker.

When at last I *did* meet him — but that is another, and far dirtier story . . .

"DOCTOR BLOOMINGTON, I PRESUME?"

or, How I Walked And Talked With The Master

It would be sheer false modesty to disclaim knowledge of the fact that the names "Bloch and Tucker" are often coupled in fandom today. Actually, they are paired so often, they sometimes sound as if they belonged together: like death and taxes, fire and brimstone, hell and damnation.

It may come as a shock to younger readers, therefore, to learn that as of 1946 — 13 years after entering fandom — I had never met Bob Tucker. Not only that, I doubt if I could have correctly identified the man.

Oh, I'd seen his name around from time to time, in various fanzines. But if you'd pinned me down, I'd have merely been able to speak of him vaguely as a "fan" along with Trudy Hemken, Walt Coslet and the little kids like damon knight and Judy Zissman.

But Fate took a hand; Fate in the somewhat unlikely form of Forrest J Ackerman. It was at his behest that I finally determined to attend my first convention — Los Angeles, 1946.

I flew out. That is to say, I flew from Milwaukee to Chicago. That was the night when TWA grounded all its planes. So I switched to a train, and the train switched around for several days. By the time of my late arrival in L.A., Ackerman had already collapsed, and I was met at the depot by eleven other fans, one of whom owned a genuine beard. No, it wasn't Sturgeon, and it wasn't Tucker either.

Tucker, however, was very much in evidence during the ensuing three days. As I recall, neither of us put in very much time during the actual sessions of the convention. But we kept bumping into each other — in such unlikely places as MacArthur Park, across the street from the meeting hall — and something clicked.

I had attended this first full-fledged fan-gathering with certain misgivings. Oh, I'd expected it to be pleasant to meet and mingle with fandom, and it was; but frankly, I thought one or two such contacts would be sufficient. But there was Tucker, and there he has been ever since. Upon meeting him, I realized that finally I had found a Purpose in Life.

It was to rib Tucker.

I had discovered a scapegoat, a whipping-boy, a target for all the concentrated malice, venom and anathema in my many-vented spleen.

Yes, thanks (or bad cess) to Tucker, I've stuck around ever since. During the past eleven years I have dutifully shown up at eight national conventions and five midwestcons, solely for the purpose of scourging Tuck.

We have shared the role of Guest of Honor; we have shared the platform; we have shared chips and ice cubes and Jim Beam and the privilege of listening to George Nims Raybin rising to a point of order. There's absolutely nothing we haven't gone through together.

Together we braved the wilds of Joliet, the fastnesses of upper Michigan, the iniquitous sinks of Chicago. Together we have gone to Niagara Falls (please be reassured, dear reader, we're not married to each other!) and avoided going to Mammoth Cave. I have invaded his home and — stretching human endurance to the uttermost — allowed him to invade mine. I have even co-edited with the man.

There is only one word to describe my sentiments as I contemplate our combined fifty years of fanning and our long mutual association.

That word is *dismay*.

THE FABULOUS MR. TUCKER

Would you write — unbeknownst to him — a life story of Bob Tucker for *Masque*? Or any one that suits your fancy. Would you, huh, would you?

— William Rotsler

The normal impulse upon seeing such a request in front of one is to move, and move quickly. Or close one's eyes and just hope it will go away.

But, why *not* write about Tucker?

I have written about Tucker before. I once did an entire article on the man's writing, artfully timing it so that it would appear just before one of his books came out. In return for a few thousand words or so of obviously lying and fulsome remarks concerning his literary ability, I received a free copy of the volume — which is just what I had hoped would happen, as I needed a doorstop.

Our bathroom door sticks.

But to move from bathrooms to Tucker, a logical enough progression, by the way, it occurs to me that neither I nor anyone else to my knowledge has ever written much about Tucker the man. Maybe because he isn't much of a man.

This is not to imply that Tucker's name is absent from the pages of fanzines or prozines, or that he has not been the subject of frequent writeups. It's merely that in almost all these mentions, Tucker has seldom appeared as or been evaluated as an individual.

Always, as my title indicates, Tucker is considered as a fabulous figure. Fabulous in the sense that a unicorn is fabulous, or a virgin.

Now this may be the proper approach. Mr. Tucker is not (and I can vouch for this personally) a unicorn. Nor is Mr. Tucker (and I *can't* vouch for this personally, but merely strongly suspect) a virgin. Nevertheless, he *is* fabulous.

The saga of his fannish exploits extends way back to 1932, and occupies almost as much space in Moskowitz's fan-history, *The Immortal Storm*, as is devoted to the story of who threw whom out of what meeting-hall. Obviously Tucker is an important figure.

Almost any newcomer to fandom soon learns a great deal about Tucker through the frequent references made to him in current journals.

They read about Tucker the letter-hack of yore, Tucker the fanzine-publisher of the Forties, Tucker the pro-writer, Tucker the hoaxer, Tucker the hoax-victim. It's all down in black and white for anyone to read. Even Tucker could read it, if his literary abilities extended beyond the mere recognition of seven letters assembled on a label so as to spell out the legend "J-I-M B-E-A-M." Incidentally, Tucker's well-known predilection for this particular beverage actually stems from his illiteracy. As an sf fan he was first attracted to the brand because he thought its name was "GIN BEAM."

So much, and not very, for the Tucker of the fables and the legends. So much for the Tucker who once tried to reach Mammoth Cave by way of Canada, the Tucker who puts the names of his friends in his books as characters, the Tucker who — at the convention in Cleveland — had to be forcibly restrained from putting up his son at the auction.

But what about Tucker the human being? A series of unfortunate accidents has caused my path to cross his through the years. We have visited one another, worked on mutual projects, travelled together, eaten together, drunk together and — I hasten to add, in all innocence — slept together. A statement which I hope will not call forth any inter-Laney-ations.

As a result, I feel that I know a bit about Arthur Wilson Tucker, and perhaps it's time fandom found out, too.

Biographically, the facts are as simple as the man himself. He was born in rural Illinois, near Peoria, on the 23rd of November. Surprising as this may seem to any number of people, the year of his birth was well within the present, or twentieth century — thus giving the lie to the rumor that Tucker is really a pseudonym of the Comte de St. Germain. The year was 1914, to be exact.

He grew up in Bloomington, went to school there and (incongruous as it might seem) in Normal, Illinois. He is a movie projectionist — but has also done work in advertising, publicity, editing, reportorial and photographic fields — plus his professional writing. In all of these fields he has managed to distinguish himself by the quality of his efforts.

For one of the apparently overlooked or unmentioned things about Tucker is that he does things well.

In a field such as fandom — a field dotted with the droppings of loud-mouthed jackasses and filled with their brayings — Tucker has always distinguished himself by the consistent quality of his efforts.

Perhaps the most fabulous thing about Mr. Tucker is that the man is efficient. He gets things done. When he started out, back in 1932, as a letter-hack and as a part-time contributor to fanzines, he made a determined effort to find a place for himself in the field as a fan. And did so, by virtue of the worth of his contributions.

As a director of various fan organizations, as an office-holder, as a policy-maker he has always offered more than mere token activity. He has been a prime mover behind many of the lasting projects in the fan field.

His success with *Le Zombie* and the *Bloomington* (later, *Science Fiction*) *News Letter* is readily acclaimed by fandom. However, many fans seem to ascribe that success to Tucker's ability as a humorist.

Actually, in my opinion, it was not the humor which elevated *Le Zombie* to the top, but the thread of candor and common-sense readily apparent in its pages. Interspersing the funny business one finds a consistent stream of authenticated news items, solid information and dispassionate editorializing. Tucker always called the shots as he saw them. And this is all the more remarkable when one considers that he did so in the days when fandom was in its infancy — its puling, brawling name-calling infancy. Any reader of the aforementioned *Immortal Storm* comes away with the impression that the fandom of *Le Zombie* days frequently resembled the government of a Central American banana republic in the 1930s — complete with feuds and revolutions and impassioned attempts at dictatorships. Against this background, *Le Zombie* rode serene in a trough of truth, steered against the prevailing winds by a cool and competent captain whose compass was not subject to erratic variation.

The *News Letter* was (and remains to this day) a model of its kind. Living up to its title in every sense of the word, it nevertheless served as a projection of the Tucker personality; a journal of opinion — *honest* opinion, objectively delivered.

Tucker is the kind of a guy who would have delighted Diogenes. He is an honest man.

Now not all fans are lantern-carriers — not all fans share the same Diogenerous inclinations. Some of them have resented, in the past, the very candor which is the keynote of the Tucker personality. Tucker is no dedicated crusader; he sallies forth Jurgenesquely without a lance. Nor does he carry a chip on his shoulder.

On the other hand (or shoulder) neither is he one to dissemble or dissimulate. If he disapproves of an individual's activities, he doesn't disguise the fact. If he is bored or tired or dissatisfied, he takes his leave of the scene — quietly, but quickly. And if he scents a sham, he is apt to speak up. Not blatantly nor melodramatically (the only time the man really lost his head was when somebody made off with his ten of clubs) but emphatically enough and bluntly enough so that the offending party is aware of his disapproval. As a result, Tucker has trod on a few sensitive toes in his time. But not, one may rest assured, through clumsiness on his part.

His cleverness, his professional talent, his extensive knowledge and background of experience in the field all contribute to his success and to his elevation to eminence in our microcosm.

But there are other clever people, talented people, experienced and learned people, who have not attained — and perhaps never will attain — Tucker's rank in general affection or esteem. Because they seemingly lack that other important characteristic; that honesty of self-expression which is so definitely a part of Tucker.

As an individual, he has always gone his own way, governing his life-pattern with the same quiet determination which marks his progress as a professional writer. He is neither a blatant exhibitionist nor a timid conformist, and the fact that this tall, crewcut figure with the almost Indian-slanted cheekbones looks a good ten years younger than he is can be attributed to clean living, the purity of Jim Beam, or a good embalming job.

All of which is not empty eulogy. It is merely an attempt to rectify a curious anomaly in present-day fandom — a situation wherein everyone writes about *Tucker* and so few people seem to know him as an individual. And as an individual, he is well worth knowing.

One final word is probably in order. It may be suspected that I am buttering up to Tucker indirectly here in case he happens to have another book published. Such is not the case.

Actually, I write this merely because I feel I owe him something. When he and his family visited us after the convention this fall, his wife fixed my daughter's bicycle.

She's a good girl, that Fern Tucker.

And if she sees something in the guy, he's got to have a few redeeming features. The mere fact that Tucker could attract so nice a female is fabulous enough for me.

Let's face it. Tucker is a good man.

THE ART OF WILLIAM ROTSLER

I do not know when the name of William Rotsler first flashed across the fannish horizon as an artist. Somebody must have the exact date — perhaps the postal authorities.

Sufficient it is to say that at this moment another great name emerged to take its rightful place alongside Van Goo, Tooloose LaDreck, Anonymous Bosh, Grandpa Breughel (not the Elder Breughel, but his father), and Ub Iwerks.

Not since the immortal Goyim painted *La Maja* has any artist displayed such a mastery of the nude. Combining the delicacy of a Boucher (not Tony you ignorant lout, but François) with the draughtsmanship of a Degas or even a Degler, William Rotsler has established a definite niche for himself in the ranks of the *Saturday Evening Post*-Impressionists.

For a while, his early work exhibited some of the massive lines of the Dutch Masters — Van Dyck, La Palina and the immortal Panatella. A later phase brought to mind the odd distortions found in the work of that unique Greek genius who painted in Spain and whose tremendous output won for him the name of El Producto.

A brief fling at abstractions found Rotsler abandoning the Cubists and taking his rightful place amongst the Squares.

And there he remains today.

His work in fan magazines has invoked the attention of numerous fen to say nothing of the above-mentioned authorities. It has lent itself, all to frequently, to glib tongue-in-cheek commentary by people like myself.

But I have waited patiently for someone to come forth and proclaim what I seriously believe to be the truth — that Rotsler is a remarkably gifted talent dealing in evocative symbolism.

Anyone privileged to have seen his compendium, *The Tattooed Dragon*, must be aware of this. His ability to recreate imagery arising from subliminal levels is almost unique in our times. Actually, when Rotsler's work is viewed as a whole, both the nudes and the noodling are all part of a pattern. He has captured and set down the ideology of the Id. Although the government will probably never commission him to do a set of murals for post office walls, it's about time all of us (including this tongue-in-cheek commentator) realized that his art is completely graphic without a hint of porno. His is the gift of insight . . . insight directed toward the hidden erotic imagery of our sexual nature, and toward the unverbalized visualizations of inner reality usually translated only through the medium of a Rorschach Test.

There are hints of this rare talent in the art of Paul Klee, Heinrich Kley, Max Ernst, George Grosz — and on another level, Chagall. Steinberg does it, and Thurber at times seems to be the Grandma Moses of this particular (and as yet undesignated) school.

But few artists have taken the direct and candid approach which is Rotsler's specialty. In *The Tattooed Dragon*, most particularly, he has managed to combine the presentation of individualized "moments of truth" with deft social (or even antisocial) commentary.

Naturally, I realize that significance, as well as beauty, resides in the eye of the beholder. But this beholder is beholden to William Rotsler for flashes of perception which are directly inspired by his unique genius.

Okay, so the word slipped out. And that means it's time for me to get back in time again, and in future to continue the great fannish pastime of making with the funnies about "Rotsler nudes."

Still, just this once, I wanted to say that I think we have something very special in our midst. And I venture to prophesy that the day will come when Rotsler will win a much wider and justly deserved recognition.

And that's when all the gagsters, myself included, are going to be proud to say, "I knew him when."

For that matter, I'm proud to know him *now*.

WILLIS IN AMERICA

Walter Willis arrived in Chicago on August 28, 1952 — I saw this catastrophe, and in the interests of fair play, for the benefit of future generations (if any) I'm forwarding this account by a bloodshot eye-witness.

Let's wander down Memory Lane, you and I, and mind you, be careful, the street cleaners haven't been around here for a long time.

I arrived at the Morrison in the early afternoon. The Morrison, for the benefit of you English cousins, is a large pub surrounded by 42 storeys of rooms. After checking in at the pub, I fell in with Messrs. Kyle and Greenberg and Evelyn Paige. They were on a similar errand . . . checking the pub to see if Willis had arrived.

The bartender hadn't seen him. So we spent several hours visiting all the neighboring pubs . . . with the same result. Obviously, Willis had not yet come to town.

Dinner was poured, and after munching down a bloater, somebody suggested checking on the whereabouts of Max Keasler. It was the cool scientific logic of the assembled pros which brought this inevitable daisy-chain of thought. The game was afoot. The plan of action, as we sketched out on the back of an old chambermaid we had lying around, resulted in the following conclusions:

(a) Where Keasler is, can Shelby Vick be far behind?

(b) Shelby Vick must be close to Bob Tucker.

(c) Bob Tucker certainly is near to Lee Hoffman.

(d) Look under the bed, and there is Willis.

Well, to make a long story cleaner, that's precisely the way it worked out. Inside of ten minutes we were hauling the recumbent form of Walter Willis out from under the bed, where he had been reading a copy of *I Go Degler*.

My first impression of him consisted of a bobbing glimpse of curly, sunbleached hair (we had just been introduced, and he was kissing my hand). His face, wreathed in ecstatic fervor, bore a striking resemblance to that of Fritz Leiber — although I didn't strike it very hard; just enough to make him stop that incessant hand-kissing.

The entire group, augmented by Bea Mahaffey, ascended the lift to my room on the 32nd floor for the ritual ceremony of preconvention . . . dropping the first bag of water out one window. Willis seemed a bit battered by his recent charabanc trip, but he kept gurgling (his lips tightly pressed around the neck of the bottle) that his first impressions of fandom, like his trousers, were ripping. In an effort to play the genial host, I produced a second bottle for the use of other members of the group, and we sprawled around and drifted into one of those pleasant discussions which make conventions so memorable — that is to say, we made derogatory remarks about everyone we could think of who was not present.

For the first time Willis displayed his remarkable wit, and if common decency did not preclude it, I'd love to include some of his funnier and more obscene comments about Harris, White, Shaw, Clarke and some of the other "---- -- -------" as he put it.

All of these drolleries, mind you, were delivered with a perfectly straight face, and while he was apparently absorbed in another fulltime occupation. (He was knitting a sweater — the one Lee Hoffman was wearing at the time.)

At half past nine or thereabouts. . . somewhere between the scotch and the bourbon, as I recall . . . the room opposite mine was occupied by George O. Smith, a little-known pro. Smith is a rather shabby specimen of huckster; loud, opinionated, given to exhibitionism (in an effort to impress onlookers, he will even go so far as to drink out of a glass) and I was a bit of a mind to conceal our presence from him. But Smith, whatever his other defects, is a keen physicist and student of electronics; and his sharp ears detected the tinkle of ice.

In three seconds flat (that's his characteristic position) he was pounding on the door and within three minutes he had moved the gathering across the hall to his suite.

I must say that my fears were unjustified. Willis took the introduction very well and behaved just as he was expected to behave — fawned, stammered, asked Smith for his autograph, told him how much he liked the *Grey Lensman* series and his "Averoigne" stories in *Weird Tales*. The rest of the evening was pleasant but uneventful — Smith had an early morning appointment and left for it just in time.

As I recall, Willis eventually went down to sleep in the lobby, as was his nightly custom (the bar closed at 2:30 A.M.).

I don't know what happened to Walt on Friday. I don't even know what happened to Friday. He might have been in the hands of Tucker and Company — fans were arriving and he probably was collecting autographs. Certainly he got a great many of the latter — by Monday night his body was completely covered with signatures. Many people commented favorably on his distinguished appearance; he looked like Bradbury's *Illustrated Man*, unless you bothered to read between the lines. How this particular gag occurred to him I'll never know, but it's typical of the man. Who else would be able to boast of sitting on John W. Campbell, Jr. for three days?

Oh yes . . . Friday evening we all had fish-and-chips at the local hostile-ry, and then just plain chips in Smith's room; chips and cards, that is.

Saturday the convention started, and from that point on things are vague in my mind. I know Willis was introduced, Willis was on a panel, Willis was witty and profound by turns. All these reports were faithfully delivered to me in the bar. Somewhere in through those days I dashed across the street with Mack Reynolds and Evelyn Paige to get a malted milk. There sat Willis, Hoffman and Keasler (who by this time were so insufferably inseparable that they were generally known as the Unholy Trinity) and it is to my credit that I persuaded Walt to drink a malted milk by convincing him that it was a glass of stout with an unusually foamy head on it.

But during the convention session proper (or improper, as the case may be) Willis was completely surrounded by massed fandom; brandishing his fountain-pen like a shillelagh and tossing off impromptu mots as fast as he could surreptitiously read them off his cuff.

My next contact with Willis was Sunday night at the banquet. Both of us occupied the speakers' table and it was my duty, in my incapacity as toastmaster, to introduce him. He delivered a positive gem of a speech on *Explorations of Space*, accompanied by slides showing Bonestell illustrations. The whole thing was masterly and came as a complete surprise to all of us. It was one of the highlights of a convention which was already well-lit.

He capped the climax later in the evening by attending the masquerade ball with his skin tinted a sensational shade of green — the inadvertent result, I learned later, of swallowing an entire ounce of the liquor being served in the Georgia Smith's room.

I saw Willis a number of times Monday — as a matter of fact, it was impossible to miss him, since every time one passed through the lobby he was lying there. Monday night the San Francisco group threw a party and it splattered all over everybody. Willis had been propped up near one of the penthouse windows and I was finally able, at long last, to get in a few moments of private conversation.

This is one of my most cherished memories . . . this midnight interlude with the *true* Willis. Soft-spoken, gentle, almost dreamy . . . he seemed a bit abstracted, true, but so sincere. I'll always remember the way he held my hand and called me "Madeleine." (Of course, some churlish fans claim he was merely so inebriated he didn't know what he was doing. This I refuse to believe. I happen to know that he was in full possession of his faculties, and sensibly held my hand in order to keep from falling out of the window.)

Tuesday I bade farewell to him, in the lobby. The stretcher paused long enough for me to gaze down at him and say goodbye. It was a touching farewell — he touched me for five bucks — and then (I'll always remember the date) on September 2nd, 1952, Willis was off — it's my guess that he still is. . . .

SECOND COMING

March 31:

AXE MURDERER SLAYS TWO IN ROW. *Details Inside*

April 1:

JESUS WALKS AS THOUSANDS CHEER
OUR SAVIOR APPEARS IN NEW YORK
JESUS CHRIST!

April 2:

CHRIST BRINGS PEACE ON EARTH IS CLAIM
NO MORE WAR SAYS JESUS
LAY OFF ROUGH STUFF SAVIOR COUNSELS

April 3:

CHRIST ON BROADWAY: TRAFFIC HALTED AS JESUS SPEAKS
MESSIAH'S MESSAGE MELTS MUGS

April 4:

SAVIOR GIVES DOPE ON VIRGIN BIRTH
IMMACULATE CONCEPTION O.K. SAYS JESUS
NINE TRAMPLED AS JESUS PREACHES IN CENTRAL PARK
MESSIAH MOBBED BY AUTOGRAPH HOUNDS
MAN WORTH WHILE IS MAN WHO CAN SMILE — JESUS

April 5:

EXCLUSIVE INTERVIEW WITH SAVIOR — J. CHRIST GIVES LOWDOWN.

NEW DOPE ON 2ND COMING. *Story on Page 2*

CHRIST NOT HERE TO START TROUBLE. DENIES SEARCH FOR POWER— YOU GOT ME WRONG BOYS SAYS SAVIOR

NO PERMANENT RESURRECTION: JUST VISITING IS PLEA OF CHRIST

PLEASURE TRIP FOR MESSIAH

April 6:

KEY TO CITY FOR J. CHRIST. OFFICIALS HONOR MASTER AT LUNCH — MAYOR SPEAKS IN WELCOME CEREMONY

CHRIST TO ADDRESS ROTARY: TURNS DOWN VIDEO CONTRACT

POPE SILENT ON JESUS VISIT

FATHER DIVINE MISSING

April 7:

CHRIST VISITS BROADWAY'S NIGHTSPOTS

SHOWGIRL SIRENS SEEK SAVIOR

BIG NIGHT FOR MESSIAH

April 8:

CHRIST WOWS WITH FIRST MIRACLE

MIRACLE FAKE IS CLAIM OF SCIENTISTS

RUMOR CHRIST WATER WALK FRAUD: HORSE-TROUGH TO BE EXAMINED

MAYO BROS. ASK AID OF CHRIST IN HEALING SICK

April 9:

JESUS LUNCHES WITH PRESIDENT

REPUBLICAN MINORITY IN UPROAR

CLAIM NEW BRAIN-TRUST: THEORY

SAVIOR APPEARS IN WALL STREET

MONEY-LENDERS BEARDED IN TEMPLE

MASTER DENOUNCES MONEY GRAB: BLESSED ARE POOR SAYS MESSIAH

CHRIST CONFRONTS COWERING CROESUSES

COMMUNIST PLOT HINTED BY MAGNATES

WHEAT HITS NEW LOW

April 10:

JESUS TO SAIL ON VANDERGILT YACHT
VANDERGILT SILENT ON PREPARATIONS FOR TROPIC CRUISE
VAN JOHNSON, RITA HAYWORTH DECLINE YACHT PARTY
IS SON OF GOD OUT FOR DOUGH?
HEIRESS HUNTING HINTED IN CHRIST CASE
JESUS FLEES REPORTERS ON PIER

April 11:

MAN OF SORROWS IN MAD ORGY ON HIGH SEAS
CHRIST STAGGERS ON WATERS
MESSIAH TAKES WINE FOR STOMACH'S SAKE

April 12:

COAST GUARD ARRESTS CHRIST PARTY AFTER WILD CHASE
IMMORALITY ALLEGED ON YACHT TRIP
I AM INNOCENT PLEADS SAVIOR
JESUS SPENDS NITE IN JAIL
CHARGES LODGED AGAINST XST

April 13:

CASE AGAINST SAVIOR QUASHED. ALL MISTAKE — VANDERGILT
SAVIOR OUT ON BAIL. CHRIST FREE ON WRIT
EXTRA — SAVIOR O.K.

April 14:

EXCOMMUNICATION RUMORED FOR J. CHRIST
JESUS LASHES CHRISTIANITY IN VICIOUS ATTACK
WILL CHURCH DISOWN BLACK SHEEP? *Story on Page 3*
CHURCH WASHED UP — JESUS
ALL THROUGH SAYS CHRIST IN INTERVIEW
FATHER FORGIVE THEM: DON'T KNOW WHAT THEY DO, CHRIST CHARGES

April 15:

JESUS SIGNED BY MOVIE MOGULS
CAST IN ROLE OPPOSITE MARGARET O'BRIEN

April 16:

MOVIE STORY ABSURD SAYS MESSIAH
NO FILMS FOR SON OF GOD
CHRIST SMASHES CAMERAS, FLEES PHOTOGRAPHERS ON AVENUE

April 17:

JESUS ANNOUNCES RETIREMENT
STRAIN TOO GREAT — CHRIST

April 18:

EXTRA! JESUS DISAPPEARS!
POLICE HINT FOUL PLAY

April 19:

NO CLUES YET IN CHRIST CASE
G-MEN TO STEP IN

April 20:

AUTHORITIES BAFFLED IN SAVIOR HUNT

April 21:

CHRIST CASE CLOSED OFFICIALLY

April 22:

AXE MURDERER SLAYS FOUR IN ROW. *Details Inside*

A PUBLIC APOLOGY

I apologize —

Because I was a cynic . . .

Because I was a skeptic . . .

Because I was a knocker instead of a booster . . . Because I was a pessimist . . . a Gloomy Gus . . . a grumbler . . . a critic . . . a cheap tinhorn liberal . . . a fool! Yes, I apologize!

When Fritz Leiber's *New Purposes* came into being, I blindly allowed myself to be misled by the phoney, sophisticated attitude of its sponsors. I admit it — I fell for their childish line completely. I heeded their sophomoric appeal for "reason and reform" in what they termed a "troubled world."

Now I can see that I was wrong. *New Purposes* is dying, and rightly so, for only one reason. It does not *deserve* to exist, for it fills no real need.

You see, I've taken another look at the world today . . . a good, long look . . . and I'm man enough to admit I was mistaken. Just take the last decade, for example. In 1940, we passed the Selective Service Act in this country . . . for only one year . . . as a protective measure. As our President assured us at the time, we would never go to war. No American boy would ever set afoot on foreign soil.

Well, lots of us so-called "wise-guys" scoffed. But it was true. No American boy was sent to foreign soil in war in 1940.

In '41 the draft continued. At the time we were told that a year or more of military training would raise national health and morale and make mature men out of the boys who were drafted. Again, we foolish doubters leered. But the years have told their own story. Many of the boys who entered service at 18 came out again as mature men of 23 or 24, only 5 or 6 years later. Figures don't lie, you know. It all came true, just as predicted.

In '42, it was freely predicted that we'd blow the enemy off the map. Well, didn't we? I pause for rebuttal . . .

In '43 we learned about our brave ally, Russia. And every year since then, we've learned more.

In '44 and '45, we were told that German military might was being utterly destroyed and that never again would such power be loosed on the world. Today, 5 years later, Germany is impotent — the Krupp works and other munitions plants are barely struggling along; the very fact that some of these institutions escaped at all and are being refinanced by American and British capital is in itself little short of miraculous.

Yes, year by year, month by month, all the optimistic predictions we were wont to sneer at are coming true. With the possible exception of Russia, China, India, Palestine, the East Indies and parts of Africa, South America and Occupied Europe, the entire world is at peace. The NAM assured us as long ago as 1945 that once odious "price controls" were removed, prices would come down and all danger of inflation would be averted. And didn't the British pound fall?

Aren't the veterans getting their benefits? Isn't Labor winning new victories on strike every day? Aren't farm subsidies helping us to produce more food, as witness the actual surplus of potatoes?

Take a good, long look about you at the world of postwar miracles. Once they were only brightly-colored advertising dreams, paid for (we nasty scoffers whispered) by government money. We didn't believe in the new world of "plastics" or the new world of "housing" or the other benefits of a new peacetime era.

But the facts speak for themselves.

Any man can go out today and build himself a $40,000 ranch type house . . . provided, of course, he has the money. (And lest some smart aleck take that as a concealed slur, let him remember that it has *always* cost money to build a home and never before could a man, if he were a veteran, get a liberal $2,000 loan toward such a project.)

And you certainly don't need very much money to enjoy that great new modern miracle of television, bringing the best of entertainment, the finest of big time sports such as professional wrestling, right into your very living room!

Yes, let us all count our blessings before we ever again dare to indulge in spurious destructive criticism. Social security . . . ballpoint pens . . . nylon shirts . . . canasta . . . popcorn in every motion picture house in the country . . . the wonderful new advances in prosthetic devices available to our boys . . .

jukeboxes so remarkably designed as to play 100 records instead of the usual 20 . . . absolutely free music and commercials provided in public transportation vehicles in many cities . . . the list is almost endless.

And in the field of modern science, witness the fight against the monster of "socialized medicine" . . . the public sale of ammoniated chewing gum and cold tablets . . . or, on a higher plane, our work in radar, jet-propulsion, rocket projectiles and atomic research.

Only four or five years ago, we marvelled at the atomic bomb. Today, such is our remarkable progress, we are already readying the "H-bomb." Not only in this country, but probably all over the world. For truly, as Wendell Willkie once said, this has become "One World."

Of course, we have not yet had the opportunity to try the H-bomb. But don't let any crackpot skeptics fool you. Our chance will come — and soon!

In the face of our magnificent present . . . and our assuredly still more glorious future . . . what can *New Purposes* offer the world?

Rest assured, mankind hasn't changed. We can still pin as much faith in humanity as we always have, and be assured of the same results.

My advice to all of you, as a retired cynic, is to count your blessings.

It might be well, however, in view of the somewhat limited time remaining, to count them damned fast!

WORST FOOT FORWARD

AUTHOR'S NOTE: Edward Wood said that he "had to laugh in Cleveland when talking to a few professionals who claimed they had seen the crash ahead of time but didn't say anything about it."

I find this interesting, because I'm one of the professionals who talked with friend Wood in Cleveland. Speaking of the sf boom and bust, I mentioned my own reaction. I said I hadn't *anticipated* the crash, but that when it came I *did* formulate a theory as to the reasons why. And I told him, and the others, about writing this article, way back in March, 1954. I showed it privately to Wilson Tucker and Dean A. Grennell, but begged off allowing it to be published at that time.

It was my feeling, right or wrong, that publication would not bring about any positive benefits — I couldn't see that it would cause a wave of reformation to sweep through the ranks of those I held responsible for sf's plight. On the other hand, I thought it might have a negative effect on the fortunes of a few of my colleagues who had managed to at least garner a few crumbs of profit. I didn't want to do this, nor create the erroneous impression that perhaps I was brave enough to sound off only because I myself wasn't profiting from the situation and thus had nothing to lose. In other words, I didn't see that the article could do any actual good, and it might unwittingly do a bit of harm.

Today I think the danger is past. The phenomena I criticize have been criticized generally by people who weren't held suspect because they might have any personal axe to grind. Consequently, I need no longer hold back because of a feeling that my opinion endangers anyone else.

On the contrary, it is probably time to speak up, for two reasons: first of all, to contribute my mite to this general effort of evaluating the problems of the sf field, and secondly, to help correct the notion — which some of the critics seem to hold — that sf operates in a sort of private universe inhabited only by publishers, editors, writers and readers and is unaffected by the world beyond. At any rate, here's what I had to say about it two years ago, and in all the reams of comment and discussion I've read since that time, I've come across nothing that would cause me to revoke or reverse my opinions.

I am writing this article in March, 1954, and it's hard to concentrate amidst the din.

That noise you hear in the background is the sound of magazines crashing, publishing houses going bust, markets exploding throughout the sf field.

If you listen closely, beneath the *fortissimo* thunder you can hear the weak, wailing counterpoint of fans and pros alike, joined in a thin chorus of bewildered amazement.

"How can this happen? Only a year ago things were wonderful; had been wonderful ever since *Destination Moon*, and getting better right along. And now, suddenly, the roof caves in. . . ."

Here's one man's answer.

It's not a pretty one, I'm afraid. It's not going to win friends and influence people. It lacks the glib references to "economic forces" and "saturation" and "distribution problems" and "publishing costs" which characterize all of the previous explanations I've heard and read.

I'm sure you're familiar with *that* gambit. It runs something like this:

"Well, you see, sf is a sort of limited-appeal proposition. Basically, it managed to struggle along for about twenty years and support three or four regular magazines and a couple of down-and-outers. And there are enough confirmed addicts to keep one or two small publishing houses going in the book market, too.

"But the minute a boom started, everybody had to get into the act. Too many magazines came out at once — too many books." And then the explanation goes into the technical pitch about "newsstand displays" and "poor distribution." And it turns out that sf is the victim of Mr. Printer and Mr. Engraver and Mr. Paper Manufacturer and Mr. Distributor. As I say, you've heard this song before. Well, I'm not here to write any new lyrics. Nor does the song itself find a place on my personal Hit Parade. I think it's a phoney. Oh, I won't deny the *facts*. They're obvious enough. It's the *conclusions* I quarrel with.

It's true that the cost of publishing anything today is inordinately high. It's true that competition is keen; that a magazine or a book is ultimately at the mercy of its distributing agent; that unless it is placed before the consumer the sales will suffer.

But these facts are not *germane* to sf alone. They apply equally to *all* forms of contemporary publication — mysteries, westerns, love stories, confessions, factual digests, "slick" magazine fiction and "serious" novels or non-fiction.

All of this material, in magazine form or in hard covers, faces the same situation.

Faces it, and (by and large) survives. The hardcover mystery finds its home in the rental library; its mass sales in a pocket book reprint. If love-stories (*sic*) are no longer published plentifully in pulp form, they have made a graceful or disgraceful transition to paperbacks. So have the westerns. The digest-sized magazines are everywhere upon the newsstands.

There have been failures, yes: the publishing field has left a trail of corpses through the years. Anyone who is rabid to refute my conclusions will undoubtedly seek to cite examples of general magazines that started out booming and ended up busting.

But, generally speaking, the overall picture is this: there are still half a hundred regular digest-sized magazines published and displayed and sold monthly on newsstands all over the country. And they enjoy a big sale. There are still scores of mysteries, suspense novels, westerns and general fiction books published for every one sf effort. Despite television, motion pictures, radio, and the delights of drug-addiction, these other literary forms continue to flourish and return a profit.

Why?

At this point, the flannel-mouths will rush in again with their previously-mentioned battle-cry. "But I already *told* ya — sf is different, see? It's like I said, a limited-appeal proposition: there ain't enough people interested to support a lot of books and magazines."

To which answer I repeat my previous question. *Why?*

Why aren't there enough people interested? If that's the case — if there is some mysterious limiting factor in our civilization which keeps the number of sf readers constant at 150,000 or 200,000 maximum — then *how* did the boom *begin* in the first place? There must have been more readers during the boom — and what starts such a boom anyway, if it's not indication of general public interest?

The answer to this one, from friend flannel-mouth, is likely to be a vague reference to "fad" and "craze" and "Well, you know how it is — these things get started for a while and then they die down again; it was just a temporary thing, on account of the movies they made and everybody talking about the atomic bomb."

(Reader, forgive me if I tend to oversimplify or vulgarize the answers I am putting into flannel-mouth's flannel mouth. I am well aware that his arguments are often couched in a much more scholarly and abstruse verbiage. I am also well aware that if I use such verbiage, it will only make me sick to my stomach. Because, basically, the answers — stripped of polysyllables — boil down to just such simple replies. Simple. And senseless.)

But let's consider that "fad" or "craze" argument for a moment. It sounds good, *until* you consider it. Then it falls apart. Every new appeal can be initially labelled as a "fad" or a "craze." The advent of *Life* as a picture magazine could have been regarded as a "fad"; interest in the first *Reader's Digest* could have been called a "craze." The fact remains that *Life* and *Reader's Digest* endured, and so did a host of imitators. The public bought and continued to buy — and the newsstand distributors found room aplenty for such magazines for this reason.

Here in the United States, during the past five or six years, another magazine form *has* risen paralleling the sf boom. I refer to the sudden appearance of a score of small women's magazines initially put out by the supermarkets but now generally sold and widely duplicated by independent publishers. During the same span encompassed by sf's rise and fall, these magazines have grown steadily in number, readership and appeal. They are not only surviving but thriving. And yet they too were initially regarded as a "fad."

Nope, flannel-mouth is begging the question, and it's about time I stopped the practice myself and got on to answers.

For some while I've been considering those answers. As a writer, my first impulse, naturally, is to throw the blame on the editors. "The damned fools haven't bought enough of my stories, maybe that's the whole trouble."

Tempting proposition, but it ain't so. I believe, by and large, that the editors in the sf field know a good deal about editing, about sf, and about the "field" *per se* and that they have admirably demonstrated that knowledge through the years.

The second impulse is to invert the proposition in masochistic self-abnegation and throw the blame on the writers. Bunch of lousy hacks, grinding out stale crud month after month.

Well. yes, to a degree. Perhaps 70% of all the published sf of the past five or six years *is* crud. But of that 70%, I'd venture to say that only 20% is unadulterated slop without any element of interest, ingenuity or intellectualization. And above the 70% is a good solid 30% of really fine writing, *superior* writing.

30%, by the way, is a high average in any field. I don't think even the confirmed mystery-story addict can truthfully maintain that 30% of all who-dunits published contain original material, literately presented. Nor are 30% of all westerns outstanding, nor 30% of the overall contents of our "slick" magazines, nor — believe me! — 30% of the annual output of so-called "serious" novels.

And the percentage of abysmal swill spewed out in these fields is markedly greater than in sf (which, by the way has consistently shown an increasing improvement year after year).

Yet these other types of fiction survive and prosper despite (by and large) much poorer writing and editing.

So I can't conscientiously blame editors or writers for the fate of science fiction today.

Well, who else is there left to crucify? How about taking a crack at the publishers? That's a popular gambit. Everybody hates those fatheads — sitting back and taking their profit simply because they have a lot of dough to put up for backing; bunch of stupid jackasses who interfere with editors and louse up the ideas of artists and writers.

Granted. But they do in every field, and prosper despite their mistakes. Sf has had its share of know-nothing publishers, of greedy publishers, of dictatorial and opinionated publishers. But no more so than the other *genres*. So, regretfully, as the sun sinks in the west, we must take our leave of publisher-land without depositing the burden of guilt. This leaves another large group: the readers. Serious Constructive Fans (the kind who used to play with Erector sets when they were kids, and who are still engaged in such symbolic auto-eroticism today) generally come up with this answer. The *readers* are the villains. They killed sf because they didn't insist on the right kind of stories. (Viz: the kind the Serious Constructive Fans enjoy.)

This is nonsense, and I have some valid arguments to prove it. These arguments are named Heinlein, Bradbury, Sturgeon, Kuttner, Leiber, Matheson, Boucher, Russell, Kornbluth, Clarke, Moore, Pohl, van Vogt, Asimov, Merril, Tenn, Gold, Simak, Bester, Farmer, Brown, Knight, Tucker, Robinson, Wilson, Wyndham, del Rey, Bixby, Leinster, Blish, Sheckley, Anderson, Dick, Reynolds, Bretnor, McIntosh, Pratt, de Camp, MacLean, Williamson, Clement, Smith, Cartmill, Neville and a dozen others.

I do not like all of these authors, myself. I do not necessarily like *all* of the writing of the authors whose work, by and large, I do enjoy.

Neither, I suspect, does any reader.

But there are, in the above list, *enough* good writers who produce, consistently or inconsistently, *enough* good stories to constitute an enviable record for the past half-dozen years. The 30% of *superior* writing previously alluded to.

And the regular readers know it, and laud the writers — their editors — and their magazines. Reading tastes in sf have measurably improved, and thus helped to measurably improve the quality of the writing.

I'm afraid the Serious Constructive Fans will have to go back to their Erector sets. We can't blame the readers, either.

So here we are. Typical whodunit situation. Who killed sf? Publisher isn't guilty. Editor isn't guilty. Author isn't guilty. Reader isn't guilty.

Can it be . . . the butler?

(NOTE TO THE PATIENT READER: If you are a smart guy, you will realize that *this* is exactly the place wherein to end this article. Just recast the whole thing in the form of a "serious inquiry" and allow the poor audience to figure out the answer. But I'm not going to play such a scurvy trick. I leave such cowardly devices to scoundrels like Walter Willis or Chuck Harris and — like the damned fool that I am — plunge recklessly ahead to stick my own tender neck out for the chopper.)

So I'll tell you who killed the sf boom. George Pal and his pals.

The popularity of sf was killed by its popularity.

And we're all equally guilty, because we all thought it was such a wonderful thing.

We cheered when Campbell's "Who Goes There?" was filmed as *The Thing*, and we gloated because it was a "success" (i.e., made money for its producer). We glossed over the first danger-signal — the very change in title itself. We excused what they did to the story. We extenuated the treatment, the corn. We said — God pity us all! — "Maybe they had to ham it up for a wider audience. The important thing is, it's sf on the screen and that's going to be a boost for the field. Others will come along and do better, wait and see."

In fact, we had already seen something that might partially justify our predictions — *Destination Moon*. Sf was now in Technicolor, yet. Dignified with an "original musical score," yet. Graced by the presence of "technical advisors," yet. Oh, granted, there were a *few* flaws and they really didn't need that formula approach to the story, but they'll improve, wait and see.

(We were willing to forget, in our naïve rapture with the wonder of it all, that some of the most unChristly westerns are in Technicolor, have their "original musical score," are blessed with "technical advisors" who instruct actors on how to get fifty shots out of a six-shooter before reloading.)

Along came the Lipperts and the Obolers and the Schtunke Brothers and a flock of shoestring independents with a half-dozen follow-up films which not even the most fervid apologist could disguise — horrible travesties. But we kept saying, "Good publicity. Good for the field. Start a boom."

And the barracuda began to swarm around the radio and TV studios — nibbling. Toss them a couple of good yarns and watch them tear hunks out of them and float the dismembered corpses onto the air. Sure, a lot of it was admittedly junk, but — "Good publicity. Sf on radio and TV now. We can't miss."

I thought the same way, as late as 1951, in New Orleans. There, as ancient withered members of Sixth Fandom can attest, the convention of that year was given preview showings of *The Day the Earth Stood Still* and *When Worlds Collide*.

The Day the Earth Stood Still pleased me immensely. Although the satraps had faithfully followed their policy of buying a story (Bates' "Farewell to the Master") and then changing it into something else, I felt they had effected an intelligent, adult transformation. No conventional love-story, no phoney adulation of present-day society as contrasted by monstrous invaders; and a generally adult treatment was manifest in the presentation. This kind of sf I personally could understand and enjoy and endorse as contributing to the stature of the field.

When Worlds Collide, however, was a horse of a different Technicolor. Or part of a horse, anyway.

The *scientist* was back. The *old* scientist and the *young* scientist. And the beautiful girl in a sweater. The one from *The Thing*, and the half-dozen other horrors. And we were off on that "end of the world" kick, with a vengeance. Technicolor was just ginger-peachy to show fires, explosions, floods and red corpuscles.

The writing, the characterization, the dialogue, were on the comicbook level. There was another "original musical score" and another group of credits to the "technical experts," but this sop could fool nobody. It was obvious that Mr. Pal (and his imitators) had found the formula. Make a picture or two and pick the brains of the schmoes (Hollywoodese for authors, artists, pedagogues, technicians and theorists who originate an idea) and then kick them aside while you go after the loot. Give 'em the old one-two. Play it for tits and titters.

And so it went, through '52 and '53. While the sf fans, the sf editors and writers for the most part (God pity them!) howled in blind approval of their own disembowelment. *Another* TV show? *Wunderschön! Another* movie? *Magnifique! Another* radio series? *Bravo!* Also *ole, banzai, skoal* and *cheers*. So the new TV show consisted of a dramatized comicstrip deliberately aimed at the 10-year-old level. Who cares? Wasn't it proof that sf was coming into the big time? So the radio program was *Captain Star* or some other such idiocy. The important thing to remember was that sf was on the air. So the movie was *Invaders From Mars* or (yikes!) *Abbott and Costello Go To Mars* — what the hell, it must be good for business.

Actually, it was good for Hollywood's business, and TV's business and radio's business. For sf it was terrible.

It's easy to see why an obscure actor like Richard Carlson would have reason to turn handsprings over this development, and why a girl like Barbara Rush would rush out and buy half a dozen new black sweaters in anticipation of *her* development. But why anyone in the sf field could rejoice in the face of what was happening is beyond comprehension.

Yet they cheered when Bradbury's *Post* yarn was filmed as *The Beast From Twenty Thousand Fathoms* — cheered because it meant one of "our boys" was making a sale. Again, good for Ray: if the ghouls are scrabbling for bodies, it's at least nice to know they'll occasionally pay the owner for the use of his cadaver. Good for Ray because he got paid — but bad for sf. Bradbury's own career went up a notch because of this, and more power to him now that he's a screenwriter and in the dough. But Bradbury the writer, Bradbury the sincere artist, certainly suffered when his story emerged as a vehicle whose plot and treatment can be capsulized in one line — and one of the hoariest lines ever exhumed — *viz.*, "Look out, boys, the monster is loose!"

And that's all the popularity of sf in mass media has been able to produce so far: one-line plots for one-cylinder brains.

If it isn't "Here comes the monster" it's "The world is being destroyed." If it isn't "Captain Fatso and his blaster" it's "Brilliant young nuclear physicist to the rescue." Nothing else. But nothing.

Probably the whole grisly business reached its apotheosis in 1953 with the production (*sic*) of *The War of the Worlds*. This was another Pal-sied effort, based on the novel by H.G. Wells. ("Based on" is another Hollywood euphemism, meaning "What the hell, the guy's dead, let's boot it around for laughs and see if we can come up with a real hot storyline.")

Well, they came up with a real hot story line. To begin with, they had Technicolor. That meant plenty of opportunity for more fires, more bombs, more explosions, more blood — the essence of sf. Cater to the sadist — the potential and actual pyromaniacs, paranoids and psychopaths in the audience who revel in fantasies of mass violence and destruction. That's the sweet mystery of life, the secret of it all: when you make a *Quo Vadis* you're under no illusions that your audience will attend because they're hot to see the story of a Roman's conversion to Christianity — you know damned well that they're paying their dough to see the Mass Orgy, the Burning of Rome, and the Bloody Arena with the Christians Thrown to the Lions.

So there's the formula, and Pal used it, of course: he's about as much interested in advancing sf as you are in early Sumerian artifacts, but he is interested in that ever-loving buck, and so are all the mass-media impresarios.

As a result, he came up with a polychromatic abortion which to my mind represents the ultimate low in so-called sf films. It had *everything*. The Brilliant Young Scientist was there, wearing hornrims in a few daring scenes when he talked Big Thoughts and (of course) abandoning them the moment he had a chance to get heroic. Within just a few moments after the film's opening, in walked Our Sweater Girl, Miss Milky Way herself. We also had a Wise Old Reverend in this one — and just to keep all denominations happy, a whole slew of ministers, priests and assorted dervishes whirling in at the *finale* when God triumphed over those Nasty Bug-Eyed Monsters that tried to invade our sacred earth.

And we had the Army too. Leave us not forget the Army. They're in most of the sf-pictures. They come up with their tanks and their guns to cope with the hellish invaders, and the tanks and the guns are never any good, but somehow this young jag scientist, see, he gets in with the top brass and helps them figure out a method at the end, or tells them God will help. And by cracky, it works! Sure, there's a lot of other scientists around, too, but they aren't important. The reason you can tell they aren't is because they're all old or funny-looking, and only the handsome hero and heroine are really hep to the nuclear jive.

The Army, though, is always worth watching. Their antics in this film were almost terrifyingly typical. First there's the Tough Guy, see? A sort of bushy-browed black Fighting Irish type, who just figures on blasting the monsters to hell; no imagination, get me? Swell soldier, just the one you'd pick if you were in a tight corner on Iwo Jima or wherever, but he ain't got the *vision* for this kind of a struggle, see? So he gets smeared.

Now don't get me wrong — we're not saying anything *against* the Army, we're not *offending* anybody. (If we did, they wouldn't let us borrow their tanks and stuff to use in our pictures.) Even when this Tough Guy gets smeared, he's still showing how brave he is, and at the last, when he can see things are hopeless (which is about 15 minutes after the dumbest three-year-old child in the audience can see it) he yells for his men to run, and gets killed.

But let's give Pal his due. He wouldn't let the Army down this way, not our sf-loving, patriotic producer! He's also got a Smart Guy. Real top brass, a general no less, and a Brain. A sort of a Heinlein-type military man; the kind of a guy who can act casual even in the face of the unknown, and rip out a word like "para-psychology" without goofing it, just to show that Military Intelligence is prepared for Any Emergency. True, he can't figure out the invaders, and after he drops an atomic bomb on them (just so the audience gets its full measure of sf's significance) he's a little puzzled — but not licked. Nosiree! He keeps right on fighting, and works out a plan to evacuate whole cities in less time than it would take for the average man to evacuate his bowels.

Meanwhile hero and heroine tangle with the monsters (which, incidentally, operate a bunch of 1927 Paul-designed machines come to life and who themselves resemble some sort of nasty spiders or insects or horrid icky bugs; uggh it gives you the *creeps* just to look at the filthy things!) and the priests pray for deliverance, and the common people (Hollywoodese for extras, bit-players and stunt-men) run around screaming and burning and getting crushed under walls.

Finally, God comes along and saves Los Angeles. (And about time, too!)

This, then, is Big Time Stuff — sf, 1953. And from advance reports, it is sf, 1954, and perhaps 1955, if the films and the TV and the radio shows continue to find an audience. There is no reason why they won't, in my opinion: the comicbook readers and the kiddies are always with us. They went for *Superman*, so why won't they go for this?

But *this* is precisely what is killing sf in the legitimate sense of the word, and in the legitimate literary markets.

It's happened before. Let's consider *Superman*, for example. The rise of the cartoon strip, along with *Buck Rogers* and *Flash Gordon* in the mid-thirties, set sf back ten years. Right after Weinbaum and Campbell and a few others started to produce literate stories, stories which fans could reasonably introduce to their friends as evidence of the good reading to be found in the magazines, along came *Superman* and his imitators — and immediately sf *per se* was identified in the mind of the general public with the hogwash of the comics.

Adult and adult-minded readers protested in vain to their friends that *this* wasn't what they meant by sf, but the friends leered. And so did the editors and critics in the mainstream of contemporary letters. Sf had to spend the next ten years under the crippling label of "comic book trash."

Fantasy fiction suffered a similar blow. *Weird Tales* and *Unknown Worlds* purveyed what is today conceded to be some pretty good yarns — again, the statement is relative, but qualitywise the average was high. Then the movies (and the radio) got off into a "horror kick" — studios like Universal began to grind out quickie bilge to a point where it became ridiculous even to them, and in self defense they started to kid the *genre* with their *Abbott and Costello Meet* series, and put Boris Karloff into burlesque.

About this time, fantasy fiction went into a decline and virtually died — killed by corn in the mass markets.

I personally have an axe to grind here: when today I find it almost impossible to get a fantasy piece published and learn that book firms are afraid to issue a fantasy novel any more.

And I wonder how many sf writers are beginning to learn, in the face of present market decline, that they have an axe to grind, too? I wonder how many of them see vulgar, imbecilic efforts like *The War of the Worlds* and mumble under their breaths, "Good Lord! How do they get away with it? Why, I couldn't sell that guff about the handsome young scientist and the beautiful gal and the wise old priest and the saved-by-the-hand-of-God ending to a half-cent-a-word market today, and yet some screen writer got more for turning out that bilge than I can hope to make, myself, with a full year of decent, honest effort."

And I wonder how many of these writers are beginning to see, as I see, that it isn't a matter of personal jealousy or a matter of wondering how somebody else "gets away" with it, but a more vital matter of what's going to happen to the field itself if this continues?

Because that's the big problem. The more popular so-called sf becomes in the major media, the less chance there is for survival of the actual *genre*.

I'm no spokesman.

I know that, and because I know that, I've waited patiently for some Big Name Author or some recognized publisher or some established editor to step forward and point out these few simple truths for the consideration of all who have a stake in sf.

But I've waited, so far, in vain. Editors seem content to castigate authors: the trouble is, authors write "downbeat stories" or they don't come up with "new ideas," so magazines aren't selling. And publishers keep moaning about "costs" and "distribution." And the Big Name Authors privately blame both editors and publishers.

None of them, to my knowledge, have been listening to the Boom — or recognizing it as the sound of their own empire collapsing.

But it's there.

Back in the twenties, the thirties and early forties, the big gripe was the Lurid Cover; the BEM and the Beautiful Heroine coming to grips month after month.

Most writers and most confirmed readers were unanimous in their opinion — these covers were a detriment to sf. They kept thousands of potential readers from ever buying a copy of an sf magazine and discovering that the contents were often way above the illustrations.

Editors and publishers patiently explained that the covers "sold" the magazines, and that, by inference, the authors were allowed a place in the pages only by sufferance.

Until finally a few daring souls actually started to produce sf magazines with conventional or at least sensibly-conceived covers — and the sales went *up!* And *up*. And *up*.

Today we're in exactly the same situation. Our sf movies and TV and radio shows are our "covers." They are the gaudy exterior which represents sf to the millions of non-readers.

Amongst those millions of non-readers are, potentially, perhaps another quarter or half or even a million future regular readers.

But all they see now are the "covers." The sickeningly trite and lurid movies, the juvenile TV and radio operas.

There is nothing here to ever attract them to the magazines. There is nothing here to suggest that sf today can offer a *Demolished Man*, a *Wild Talent*, a *More Than Human*. The mere fact that some of the Big Name Authors have lent their *names* to the mass media does not mean they have been allowed, as yet, to lend their creative ability.

And the result is woefully apparent.

Once more sf is being equated with BEMs, bras and bushwah; the mills of the Gods are grinding corn.

Certain of my fellow sf writers have at times pointed out a hideous irony: actual scientists achieved the techniques of nuclear fission and then turned them over to the military; perfected innovations like radio and television and turned them over to the dollar-hungry horde of commercial advertisers for their profit.

Well, here's another irony: my fellow sf writers have created a literary medium and turned it over to the Big Wheels without a whimper — and are being themselves victimized thereby.

Oh, like all generalizations, there will be exceptions. A lot of them, I hope — albeit wistfully. Maybe we'll have a few more pictures like *The Day the Earth Stood Still*, or better. Maybe a lot of them. Heaven knows, we need them badly.

Certainly, the other fields have a glut of poor material which has won them condemnation from many quarters. But the mystery and detective markets, despite the damage wrought by poor material, has also profited from certain outstanding efforts — *The Maltese Falcon, The Asphalt Jungle*, the earlier *Thin Man* series, radio and TV stints like *Dragnet*, well-contrived shockers such as *Night Must Fall*, etc. The westerns have lured a more intelligent audience with items like *Stagecoach*, *The Oxbow Incident*, *High Noon* and *Shane*.

This means, in terms of fiction, that there is a dual market in these other fields; a group of fairly discriminating readers for the well-written items, and a large army of hammerheaded Hammerites and hopped-up Hopalongers for the corn.

But sf has, thus far, been unable to achieve a working dichotomy in this manner. What we have, instead, is a sort of schizophrenia; on one hand a literature which is consciously striving to improve in content and presentation, and on the other, a "cover" in the form of lurid and moronic movies, TV and radio which caters only to the oafish and the perverted.

As previously stated, there is nothing in the "cover" material which could possibly lure intelligent audiences into reading the magazines. The magazines can't *hold* the audience types who enjoy the world-rapes and monster-baiting of the mass media.

Hence the phenomenon of sf's brief boom and subsequent collapse. The first films, the first programs, naturally stirred up a dither in the bosoms of the besotted: they went galloping down to the newsstands and picked up magazines. It's not an instantaneous reaction, remember — it's something that occurs to certain segments over a period of many months or several years; a "sampling" process. That's what happened. During the past three years, inspired, incited and inflamed by what they saw and heard, the louts bought magazines. They bought one, maybe switched to a second or a third. And quit. Quit cold, because the magazines didn't offer the same sort of bilge. And as they forsook their sampling and returned to the comic books, the market fizzled.

This is my opinion, yes, and *only* my *opinion*; in support of it, however, I can offer some years of experience in the field of retail advertising, where consumer wants and consumer reaction is studied in gruesome and repulsive detail.

Remedies?

Obviously, it's an either/or proposition. *Either* sf as a literary form must prostitute itself completely and shamelessly to the 1930-vintage space opera, *or* it must somewhere find a spokesman in high places who will improve the "covers."

I'm not condemning the present producers: it is not my purpose to excoriate

Messrs. Pal, Lippert, Lopert, *et al*, or their adapters and rewrite crews who translate story material in terms of *hoke, ham, gimmick* and *gizmo*. Nor would I even imply criticism of the few fortunate *freres* in the field who have managed to profit by selling to the mass media. They are not responsible for what happens to their work in the translation to coprolalia.

But the fact remains; sf writing in the magazines suffers for want of the proper audience because sf has been given a black eye in the mass media. It has fallen into the hands of commercializers who don't give a solitary damn about the material they are dealing with — they're "in business to make money" and that's the nature of the beast (from twenty thousand fathoms or anywhere else). These tycoons have discovered a low-budget gold mine and a simple formula — slap out some "technical effects" and hire a bunch of nonentities as performers and you're off to make a fortune.

It's about time that people who profess to have the welfare of the field at heart took a good hard look at this situation. It's about time they overcame their naïve delight in the marvels of trick photography and smothered their ecstasy at being allowed to rub elbows with real live producers and actors. It's about time they stopped exulting whenever a ham uses an echo chamber to intone, "The Earthmen must be destroyed!" and another ham on a regular mike answers, in an imitation Peter Lorre voice, "Yes, Master!" It's about time they realized the simple semantic fact that sf as they know it and enjoy it has nothing to do with sf as it is presented to mass audiences; that the success of the latter in its present guise can only continue to injure the progress of the former.

Either that, or it's about time they abandoned any pretense of interest in "raising the level" and deliberately went after the swag. And let me emphasize one thing clearly: in my opinion *you cannot do both*. There is no successful aesthetic or commercial compromise: the movies and TV and radio know it, but apparently some of the editors and publishers don't. They have, consciously or unconsciously, taken to experimenting on the sly: trying to run lurid covers and keeping the story-content inside on a high plane or, conversely, presenting an intellectual front while they subtly slant their material along the same happy-ending and God-bless-democracy-and-technology lines as the movies. This fools nobody more than once. More important, it pleases nobody. The droolers aren't content with just covers — they want to slobber over contents as well. The more literate and discriminating reader soon tires of the sweetness-and-light pap, no matter how sophisticated the presentation. This is a hard truth, and it is being learned the hard way. But if sf wants to attract the same readership as *The Caine Mutiny* and *From Here to Eternity*, it had better learn that these books never achieved popularity by presenting the Navy and the Army in Rotarian ideology ("don't knock — boost," etc.) and that the readers of those books are not necessarily all of a breed who can be lulled to sleep over and over again with the same old lullaby about how wonderful Science (*sic*) will be in the future.

I am not arguing a point here: I am merely citing an observable phenomenon. It's happening, and the results are apparent.

The book and magazine field will have to choose. Art-for-art's-sake or dough-for-dough's-sake. Both courses are equally honorable and understandable according to contemporary values. But the choice must be made in order to survive.

If it's literature, sf will have to find a few John Hustons and Stanley Kramers and John Fords who will film some first-rate material and thus attract sufficient readers to the first-rate magazines. As it is, Campbell's *The Thing* certainly won't attract permanent fans for Campbell's *Astounding*.

On the other level, it's up to the magazines themselves — those who see no hope of better circulation through running better stories would do well to cease the mental strip-tease with their artistic conscience and go all out for sex, sadism and Little Ronnie, the Boy Who Wants With All His Heart To See Mars, in hopes of picking up and holding the mass audience.

If not, the slump will continue. Continue until sf takes its former place as a very minor writing form, with half a dozen magazines, a couple of "flyers" now and then, a trickle of books and anthologies, and an occasional crumb from a critic who's hard up for a topic or wants to attract attention by his iconoclasm.

There'll still be publishers, editors, writers and fans — but not so many as the enthusiastic would wish. There'll still be some money to be made and some satisfaction in doing a good job — but not as much as is desirable.

I'm no prophet of doom. I'm not even a qualified commentator. I merely seek to explain something which, it appears to me, should be fairly obvious — and which, for some reason, everybody tries to avoid seeing or admitting. I say again, everyone makes his own choice. But it must, or should be, a sane choice, based on existing facts. If some of us want to be successful aesthetes and make money publishing, editing, or writing "good, sound sf" we'd better realize that we'll never make money unless we attract a *permanent* audience for this sort of material — and the only way to do that is have this sort of material presented *via* TV, radio and motion pictures. If some of us merely want to make money, period, we'd better come off this "raise the standards" kick and get down there in the arena and fight with the same weapons and the same tactics — using all the blood, guts and busts in our arsenal.

But heaven deliver me — and heaven deliver the field — from the schizos who try to do both; who think they can compromise with their material in an attempt to compromise the customers. As it is, the better magazines must suffer a minimal circulation — they have no spokesmen in high places: the poorer magazines are half fish and half fowl and satisfy no one, including themselves.

Blame? No one's to blame. It's a situation which has arisen — and fallen — because of individual circumstances, because we all work at cross-purposes, and seldom stop to analyze consequences. And as I say, we're not heading for actual extinction, just a mild decimation. A remnant will survive: the minimal market remains and will even enjoy a small resurgence. And let's not even rule out the possibility that the *good* material I spoke of will actually appear and save the day.

As it was, we had our boom, such as it was. But it could have been, conceivably, so much better, if we hadn't let the Big Money take over and put our worst foot forward. . . .

JUST A GODDAMN HOBBY . . .

"What's wrong with fandom as a way of life?"

— Vernon L. McCain, *Psychotic* #19

This question isn't an easy one to answer. I'd say where fandom falls down (through no fault of its own) is in the matter of what for lack of a better term we must call *relationships*. Fandom is not a homogeneous unit: taste-wise, chronology-wise, in terms of economic status or geographically.

Taste-wise, as in the case with other hobbies, it tends to fall into minute divisions which become cliques. Just as in philately, the U.S. collectors have little in common with general collectors, the cover specialists don't usually associate with lovers of British Colonials, the beginners seldom traffic with the mint completist gang — so in fandom there is this disparity in interests within the field. It is so absurd to think that all "sf fans" will get along on the basis of their specialized interests as it is to assume that an ardent Kentonite will necessarily feel kinship with the ardent Guy Lombardian; though both, in the mind of the outsider, may be considered "jazz enthusiasts."

Chronology-wise, the obvious differences are even more apparent. For the sake of argument, let us assume that 15-year-old high school students and 30-year-old housewives and 45-year-old engineers and 60-year-old businessmen can attain a certain consanguinuity or even temporary intimacy as members of an audience at a convention, or in some instances as correspondents. But in "social" situations the attitudes are bound to clash.

In terms of geography and economics, still other problems are easily recognized. The geographical problem ties in directly with the minute quantity of individuals constituting fandom — as McCain says, "at any given time probably not over 200 are active." With the result that a fan such as McCain feels himself to be damnably isolated in Idaho, and cannot make fandom a "way of life" in any even partially comprehensive sense of the term. Only a fortunate few have the privilege of choice in this matter — and once again the age factor of associates enters into it, plus the economic circumstances.

Economic-wise, we find the biggest obstacle to present-day fandom. If you read Moskowitz's *Immortal Storm* or delve through fannish history and reminiscence, one thing will become almost immediately apparent: 90% of the fans of the '30s and early '40s were in the same boat, heading up the same creek, and suffering from the same lack of paddles.

Fandom was, for a long time, a poor man's game — or a poor youth's game, to be more exact. The number of affluent fans was limited: early accounts abound with instances of hitchhikers, meal-scroungers, loans and indebtedness, shoestring conventions and economic crises. From this background springs the myth of the Dirty Pro and the Filthy Huckster — a Big Man who earns $200 or in some cases perhaps even $300 a month. And in depression days, some did, considering this to be Big Money — whereas many fans earned nothing, or had jobs affording them from $15 to $35 a week. But there was a pretty general leveling effect, economically speaking, and as a result many fans did enjoy a somewhat similar environmental background and their tastes in "private life" were conditioned accordingly.

Not so today. Today, to speak frankly, most fans earn more than a good 80% of the fulltime pros: some fans are quite well-fixed — and others are still impoverished. Naturally this affects taste and outlook and tends to create a gap in relationships. I'm not speaking now of jealousy or envy (there is, surprisingly enough, damned little of that apparent in fandom) but of the natural consequences of an economic breach. Your economic "way of life" may be limited to beans and bacon; that of your fellow fan may be geared to Steak Chateaubriand. The age gap accentuates the possibility of economic hiatus, with resultant lack of common value-patterns.

All of which is more or less self-evident. But not I'm afraid, to the earnest neofan who has boned up on his Moskowitz and his *Fancyclopedia*, and wonders why it is that he isn't invited to all the private parties at conventions or even after club-meetings — why he can't just hitch-hike across the country and drop in without warning on every BNF to stay a while — why he can't announce he's holding a regional con or putting out a brand new fanzine and get immediate cooperation from anyone he contacts.

Such depression-born phenomena scarcely exist, or can exist under present circumstances. And for this reason the "way of life" that McCain speaks of is largely impractical. Truthfully, it is also *illogical*, I believe. The trick seems to be to select a certain *aspect* or *facet* of fandom and utilize it as a hobby — for fandom by its present nature is more or less a collection of hobbies than a single, unified one. There are, as you know yourself, many fans who love to publish fanzines but wouldn't find themselves as happy attending conventions or speaking before an audience. Others are primarily correspondence conscious — still others are great joiners and club members — some like intrigue and politics — we have the Serious Constructive and the Frivolous Destructive — and every combination and permutation of same, with the further distinctions imposed by taste, age, locale, and pocketbook. For these reasons I don't recommend fandom as a "way of life." But as you and I and McCain know, it can be a very pleasant by-way.

THE COMMUNIST

I took a good look around before I went in, to be sure nobody was following me. Apparently the coast was clear, but you've got to be careful.

Snow was coming down and the streets were utterly deserted. I went into the bar and closed the door behind me, letting the grateful warmth come up as I waited for the steam to clear from my glasses.

Apparently I was the only customer tonight. Nobody came here when there was a District Meeting, and that's what I'd counted on. The bartender gave me a funny look — he must have been wondering why I wasn't over at the Armory with the rest of them.

I walked up to the bar and stood there.

"What's yours?" he asked.

"Make it straight," I said.

"Wash?"

"Blood."

He stared and leaned over, "What type?"

"702," I told him.

Now it was his turn to look around. He put his mouth close to my ear. "In back here," he murmured. "Thought you was never coming."

"How is he?" I asked.

The bartender shrugged. "I dunno. I haven't been down for a while. Last time I looked, not so good."

"Drinking?"

The bartender nodded. "Whaddya expect?"

"Think he can make it if I bring the car around?"

"Dunno. See for yourself. Come on, now, hurry before somebody comes in. Damn Security was around about six."

I stiffened. He put his hand on my shoulder. "It's all right. They didn't notice nothing." He stopped, raising the trapdoor in the floor under the back-bar. "Here you go — take the flashlight. I'll give you the office three times with my foot, like this, if anybody comes in."

He stamped in demonstration as he handed me the flashlight. I clicked it on and clambered down the steps as he closed the trapdoor over me.

I went down the short passageway and opened the cellar door. It wasn't the regular cellar — just a room hollowed out behind the coal bin, I guess. Hardly the place to spend the weekend, and its single naked light bulb, dim and dangling down over the table, the chair, the cot and the toilet.

The big man stood up when I came in. That is, he tried to stand up, but he couldn't quite make it. He trembled a little — but that might have been the whiskey, too. I could see the empty fifth-bottle on the floor and the half-filled one resting next to his right hand. If that wasn't evidence enough, I had only to look at his eyes. They were rolling around in the sockets like a couple of bloodshot marbles.

"Hello," I said. "All ready to go?"

He gulped. "Jesus, you frightened me when you came in. Thought it was —"

I nodded. "Nothing to worry about. Everything's set."

"But they said this afternoon some time —"

"I got held up. Or rather, we couldn't find our pilot. This isn't exactly the night for a trip to Canada, you know." I smiled at him. "But we're all straightened out now. Got a car down the street, take you right to the field. He thinks he can make it if he gets above the storm — he's taken off without lights before."

"Field?" He gulped again. "That's dangerous, isn't it?"

"Everything's dangerous. But you can't expect him to risk the airport. You packed?"

He glanced down at a battered briefcase. "Sure. All I've got."

"Don't worry. There's some money waiting for you in Winnipeg. And a job."

"Organization?"

I hesitated. "Well, not exactly. I mean, we know what you've been through — we figured you ought to rest up for a while before trying any more writing. A couple of months at some routine job in a store ought to put you back in shape."

"Sure. That's what I need. Little rest." He reached for the bottle.

"Better hurry," I told him. "You're expected."

"Just one more." He tilted the bottle, passed it to me. "How about you?"

I shook my head. He looked at the bottle, started to set it down, then raised it again. "Cold outside," he said. "Better have another for the road."

"For the road." I noticed the scars on his neck when he put his head back to drink. I guess they beat him up pretty bad. He caught me staring at him and said, "How's Tuck?"

I didn't answer.

"What's the matter?"

I sighed. "You know we can't talk. The minute we start exchanging information —"

"Yeah, I know. But I been out of touch for so long. Did you ever hear what they did to Campbell?"

"Please, you know I can't tell you."

"But damnit, I want to know! I got a right to know!"

"Nobody has rights any more," I said. "Just duties."

"Quit stalling," he wheezed. "I'm no kid. I can take it. I know what happened to Hank and Kat and to Fritz and some of the others in town here. Hell, I was there when they got Bea —"

"Forget it," I said. "Let's go."

He reached for the bottle again. "You!" he said. "You act like you were in Security yourself. Won't talk, won't tell a guy anything —"

I leaned over and took the bottle out of his hand. "Look," I murmured. "You've had enough."

"Sure. I've had enough." He grinned, and I could see the black crevice of his mouth, and the place where they'd knocked his lower teeth out. "I've had enough sitting in cellars, waiting and watching and wondering. I've had enough of this 'forget it' stuff, too. You think a man *can* forget? God knows, I tried. But liquor's no good, and when I sleep the dreams come, and then I'm back there at the Hearing and they're working me over, asking me about the magazine —"

"Come on," I said. "You can sleep on the plane. Tomorrow morning you'll be in Winnipeg, ready to —"

He shook his head. "Ready to what? I'm not ready for anything any more. I ought to be locked up, with the rest of them, or down under with George O. and Mel and Ted and Judy."

"Don't talk like that," I said. "We're still fighting."

"Fighting? How — and what for? Sending out those damn mailings from Canada. You know the post office confiscates half that stuff — the Censor

Division has it all spotted. And what if it gets through? Half the people on our lists are dead. The other half won't be around long either if they're ever caught reading what you send. Who the hell does Phil think he is, anyway — Tom Paine? You can't start a revolution by mail. And who wants one around here? People like Security."

"You're just tired. You'll talk differently after a rest."

"No." His hand went to the bottle again. "Don't try and stop me. It's no use. I made up my mind."

"Please, we must go now —"

"I made up my mind, I told you. I'm not going."

"But —"

"Sorry. I know you went to a lot of trouble, you and the whole Movement. But I'm not worth saving anyway."

"Of course you are. Why, you're one of the Big Names, look at what you've done."

"You look at it. If you can find anything to look at." He laughed, burbling into the bottle. "Sure, I wrote a lot. Edited, too. Used to go to all the conventions. You remember those conventions, Bob?"

"Sure," I said. "I remember."

"Thousand people. We had a thousand people at Chicago. And Philly and Frisco — remember how Jerry used to play the piano? And this guy Ed Wood, we used to sit there and argue about —" He slammed the bottle down. "Ah, to hell with it! What's the use of thinking about the past?"

"Now you're talking," I said. "We've got to think about the future."

"No you don't!" He leered drunkenly. "'Gainst Security to remember? When their damn Committees figured out it was subversive — all this stuff about space travel and rockets. Said we were prying around in Top Secret information. Then they stopped the magazines and the books and they got after the fan org'nizations. Said they were 'all Communist fronts.' Said we were all Communists, too. Big laugh, isn't it? But they proved Orwell was, and then said Huxley and H. G Wells and Russell and all the others had Commie ideas — so that made us Commies too. And with this war scare and everything —"

I glanced at my watch. "We haven't much time," I said.

"We haven't *any* time. Our time ran out long ago." He sloshed the last inch in the bottom of the bottle, then drained it. "Time ran out for Acky and Doc and Cliff and all the boys. I saw a picture of Marty after they got through with him —"

He began to shake now, and I saw that he was crying. "We never hurt anybody," he said. "We did our best, and if Bradbury wrote about burning books he never figured it would make trouble. Ray wasn't any Communist, nor Horace and Evelyn, nor Sam. It was all right until after election and then they got tough."

"But you can't take it lying down," I told him. "We've got to fight as best we can."

"There's no fight left in me," he whispered. "Not after the Hearing, not after they confiscat'd everything and tossed me out, and they did what Ray said — they burned the books, they burned the house, they burned all my manuscripts, that novel I was writing, they burned it and they might as well burn me too —"

I looked at my watch again.

"Go ahead," he murmured. "Shove off. I'll be all right. Tell them to save some other poor sucker. Matheson, maybe, or Sturgeon — oh, I forgot what happened to Ted. Tell them not to worry about me. I'll be leaving here tomorrow."

"You're sure that's the way you want it?"

"I'm sure." He waved his hand. "Good-bye. And goo' luck!"

"Good-bye," I said.

I went out, closed the door, and climbed the steps. Then I tapped on the trap-door. The bartender let me out. The place was still deserted.

"Where is he?" asked the bartender. "What happened?"

I told him.

"But what'll I do with him?" he sighed. "If he's in the shape you say he is, he's liable to go wandering around shooting off his mouth and —"

It was my turn to sigh. Sigh, and think of the past; of who he had been and what he had been to me, of the times we had together in the old days. And then it was my turn to forget it. Forget it, and tell the bartender, "We'll be sending somebody around. Earl, or maybe Frank Robinson. Got to do it — it's the only way."

"Guess so."

"There won't be any trouble," I said.

"Right."

I went to the door. "Have another customer for you one of these days. But in case I don't see you beforehand, Happy New Year."

"Yeah," said the bartender. "Happy 1965!"

THE DEAD-BEAT GENERATION

I'm tired of rebels without causes. I'm tired of a Beat Generation that never had the guts to put up a fight. I'm tired of their antics and their exhibitionism, tired of all their four-pound books containing four-letter words. I'm tired of their continual attempt to hoist a new flag over American literature — a national emblem in the shape of a dirty T-shirt.

It all started, I suppose, when Ernest Hemingway picked his first bum up out of the gutter, gave him a shave and a haircut and introduced him into polite literary circles as the New Hero. Here was army-deserter and nurse-seducer Frederic Henry, and then Jake of *The Sun Also Rises*, whose impotence — real, and symbolic — reduced him to getting his kicks from drinking bouts and bullfights. Hemingway's Lost Generation foreshadowed the Beat Generation in many respects (to say nothing of disrespects) in that none of them ever seemed willing to take on any responsibilities. None of them, for example, had any use for marriage except for Harry Morgan in *To Have and Have Not* — and he was wedded to an ex-prostitute, which apparently extenuates him. Again, none of them exhibited much success in holding a job — with the exception of the aforesaid Harry Morgan, who engaged in illegal smuggling activities. The Hemingway hero was a man who lived for violent sensation; for what is known, in today's jargon as "kicks."

Then came John Steinbeck, who started a sort of literary Salvation Army for the benefit of the dispossessed; the economically and socially underprivileged. It is generally conceded that he beat the drum and passed the tambourine in a worthy cause during the first years of his mission. But pretty soon the missionary decided to join the cannibals. Steinbeck took off his clothes and turned savage. In *Tortilla Flat*, *Cannery Row*, and *Sweet Thursday* he preaches a new gospel. Only the bums are worthy of salvation. If you earn a dollar, you're a conformist and a rat; if you *steal* it, you're a Natural Man and enjoying the Good Life.

Naturally, both Hemingway and Steinbeck saw little harm in sexual promiscuity, but it remained for a host of imitators to take the next logical step and proclaim that while seduction of virgins is fun and bedding with bawds even more so, the best role is that of pimp.

It's probably no accident that the protagonists of *From Here To Eternity* were, respectively, an army sergeant who seduced the wife of his superior officer, and an enlisted man who deliberately set about to carry on an affair with a fulltime prostitute, deserting the army to live on her earnings. More of the roots of this sexual philosophy are visible in James Jones' *Some Came Running.*

Jack Kerouac and other contemporary writers have added the refining touches of mooching, freeloading and drug addiction to the catalogue of heroic activity. But it remained for Nelson Algren to integrate the whole credo in a whole series of vaguely repetitious books which reached their ultimate synthesis in the much-praised *A Walk on the Wild Side*. It will pay us to briefly examine this masterpiece in order to see just what kind of a hero we're dealing with.

Dave Linkhorn, true to the American Dream, is a poor country boy without much formal education. He begins his climb to man's estate by bedding down with a Mexican woman some years his senior. When she discovers that he is raiding the cash register while in her employ, he forcibly rapes her in the back yard in broad daylight and hops a freight for New Orleans. En route, he encounters (in every sense of the word) a teenage female tramp who assists him in robbery until confronted by the police; whereupon our hero deserts her and flees. Reaching New Orleans, he indulges in amorous adventures with floozies of all races, colors and creeds (for his is the true spirit of Democracy) and embarks upon a series of questionable enterprises ranging from smalltime con-games to bigtime manufacturing of contraceptives. But before long he has grown in wisdom and maturity to the point where he reaches the logical goal of any Modern American Hero — he becomes not only a panderer but a stud performer in a peepshow exhibition. He crowns his career by running off with the prostitute girlfriend of a legless cripple; the latter eventually beats him up and blinds him. Whereupon he returns to his home town and, presumably, his first mistress.

Now it would be easy to claim that Mr. Algren is merely presenting here a Slice of Life — a sort of raw hero sandwich. But there's a pickle in the middle and an onion on top; a liberal garnish of the author's sentiments regarding his character and situations. Again and again we find an echo of the philosophy of all the "little magazine" writers of the Thirties whose hearts bled for the bums and froze for the bourgeoisie. Only it's carried far past the Left, way over to the Other Side of the Law, where the motto, scratched on the jailhouse wall is, "Only Saps Work." And that's the motto emblazoned in the literary firmament today.

All across the American literary scene below we find the Me-Firsters in the saddle, riding roughshod over every semblance of common decency. The torn-shirt brigade, led by Stanley Kowalski, shambles across the American stage; the hep cat brandishes his switchblade on the screen; the uncouth youth is glorified in song and story, and the moron of yesterday is the Man of the Hour. The late Robert M. Lindner coined the title, *Rebel Without a Cause*, for his case-history of a criminal psychopath. It remained for popular fancy, ironically enough, to transfer that title to a movie which glorified the self-pitying exhibition of destructive tendencies on the part of a juvenile delinquent.

Through everything runs this self-pity; this weeping and wailing and disclaiming of all personal responsibility; this sniggering contempt for the "squares" and the "creeping meatballs" who obey the rules and heed anything except the need for immediate sensory gratification at any cost. They are not even granted the right to exist; they are "nowhere." Whereas the "hip" characters, of course, are "out of this world."

Contemporary literature glorifying the self-labelled Beat Generation has also managed to identify with the so-called Jazz Cult. Now I'm not knocking the sound, man, but jazz is a sound. It is not a Way of Life, embracing snobbish disdain of "mouldy figs" or sneering contempt for those who don't dope, drink and debauch themselves into an early grave. The metaphysics of music may or may not have a meaning for Albert Schweitzer when he plays Bach — but I am somewhat dubious of the drunken lout who stands in a bar, waiting for an opportunity to steal the change from a befuddled customer, and meanwhile rhapsodizes over the "inner meaning" of the New Sound. And I'm tired of reading about his hangovers described in terms of Promethean agony; tired of Hamlet's Soliloquy about whether or not to "kick the habit"; tired of "jumps" and "kicks" and "blows" and "flips" and all the rest of the acrobat's vocabulary used to describe the antics of adolescence. I'm weary of "bugged" and "dragged" and "beat" heroes who have replaced the load of conscience with a monkey on the back.

The catch-phrases of Zen and Existentialism are no substitute for a philosophy genuine enough to provide a way of life; literary "name-dropping" means nothing in books written with a profound disregard, not to mention ignorance, of form and style; growing a beard may do wonders for a weak chin but cannot hide a weak intellect. The lack of disciplined imagination, disciplined talent, disciplined thinking, is everywhere apparent. For my own part, I'm willing to join in the chorus invoked against certain forms of discipline — military, political, theological, or sociological. But if one rejects these, one must perforce substitute another form in their place; a *self*-discipline which is necessary to the integrity of the artist in his role, both as a creator and as a human being.

And that's the real point. If it were merely a matter of personal preference, I could gladly hold my peace. But we are, most of us, in general agreement that literature is a mirror of our times — and what a cracked and dirty mirror is held up before us by the Deadbeat Generation of writers; what a reflection cast upon all of us!

We pretend great alarm over the deadly "psychological influence" of comic books, but no comic-book monster or villain pauses in mid-panel to deliver ponderous monologues justifying his atrocities; nor does the cartoonist step in to offer a profound *apologia* for his antisocial depravities.

We profess a disdain for many so-called "cheap pocket-books" because of their "tough guy" protagonists — but in almost every instance, the errant character is shown paying the penalty for his misdeed, without any crocodile tears being shed by the author. Speaking for myself, when I deal at any length with an antisocial, overly aggressive protagonist, I explicitly emphasize that psychotic irresponsibility does not lead to happiness, and that no matter how much he rationalizes, a rat remains a rat.

And yet when we come to Literature — with a capital "L" and a pricetag of $3.95 and up — we encounter this endless glorification of the Slob. Moreover, the authors and critics seem to have created a new in-group — the *slob-snobs* — who are dedicated to the idealization of the Village Idiot and the worship of the Professional Heel.

It's no longer merely a matter to be left in the hands of abstract critical opinion; not at a time when we as a nation are so desperately in need of friendship and understanding in the world abroad. Thousands upon thousands of present and potential opinion-leaders in foreign countries are reading American novels today in an attempt to gain increased "understanding" of our people. Naturally they are prone to seek out the "best" in current fiction. What sort of a notion of national character and philosophy do they derive from a reading of *On the Road, Some Came Running* or the prize-winning *A Walk On the Wild Side*?

More important, at a time when our own leadership has belatedly and reluctantly recognized the need for encouraging education and integrity amongst our youth, what service is being performed by a literature which offers, as its *heroes*, an endless procession of self-centered, self-pitying moochers and lechers, "cool cats" wailing endlessly for "kicks?"

Any psychotherapis,. anthropologist, or sociologist can tell you the importance of the "hero role" in our folk-culture and show how we choose our national symbols.

It is not my intention to plead for censorship. True censorship can come only from the creative intelligence itself, and it must come now from the Deadbeat Generation of writers who have done their best to dethrone Tarzan and elevate the Ape.

The danger in selecting the wrong national symbols is by no means an empty one. Not too long ago, within the memory of most of us, a confused and restless group of young men — self-styled Rebels Without a Cause, and self-identified members of a "Lost" or "Beat" generation — found just such a symbol around which to unite; first on a *literary*, and then on a *national* and *political* level. And their symbol, too, was just such a pimp as is presently proclaimed a hero.

His name, in case you've forgotten, was Horst Wessel.

CAUSE TO READ JOYCE

To be a professional critic is to be professionally fickle. As old First Fandom member Robert Browning once remarked, "A man in armor is his armor's slave," and anyone arrayed in the breast-plate and cuirass of criticism must willy-nilly follow the critical Code of Unchivalry.

It is one of the tenets of that Code, apparently, never to praise today what you praised ten years ago — and always to openly disparage what you exalted in the still more remote past. There are, of course, exceptions to this rule; these exceptions are known as "revivals" and consist of six-month periods following the reissuing of books by authors safely dead and done for.

On this side of the Pond we have had several such "revivals" in recent years. One centered about F. Scott Fitzgerald, and his case is so typical I might as well cite it to cover the entire phenomenon. Fitzgerald was a Boy Wonder in the early Twenties, who wrote about the wealthy youth of the Jazz Age. For a decade he was in vogue, then with the coming of the depression the critics turned on him and, true to their Code, demolished him utterly. All his previously-proclaimed virtues were found to be vices. Fitzgerald found a job in Hollywood, produced his best book (*Tender is the Night*) and began an even better one (*The Last Tycoon*) and died a dozen or so years later. He was a bitter, disappointed man; but not defeated, although critical barbs wounded him deeply. A memorial collection, containing the unfinished portions of his last book and some short stories, attracted little attention.

But after he was safely interred for a number of years, another writer did a thinly disguised biographical novel, *The Disenchanted*. Budd Schulberg, the author, had worked with Fitzgerald in Hollywood and used his experiences in the story. He produced a moving and powerful book. At the same time, a collection of Fitzgerald's stuff was published, and the movies saw fit to make a singularly inept version of his old novel, *The Great Gatsby*.

Schulberg's novel, the republished collection and the movie started one of those brief "revivals" I spoke about. Suddenly the critics "rediscovered" Fitzgerald. Articles and essays were written in praise of his work. There was much damning of the "fools" who had ignored his genius during the period of his final obscurity — and since some of the writers were these selfsame "fools" they also carefully ignored the fact that they had ignored him. For about six months Fitzgerald was elevated to the Great Hierarchy of American Letters, to reign along with Ernest Hemingway, Thomas Wolfe, Mickey Spillane and Richard S. Shaver.

But true to tradition, the critics forsook Fitzgerald again about six months later and he is now one with the forgotten hordes.

The reason for citing the above example is obvious. First of all, I wanted to scare off all Serious Constructive Fans, to whom a discussion of anything outside the field is anathema. Secondly, I wanted to attempt to establish the singular nature of critical appraisal as currently practiced — in order that the reader can safely dismiss the pretensions of omniscience common to critical pronouncements.

I have yet one other example to furnish before plunging into the theme of this dissertation, and I'll make it brief. I refer to the case of Ernest Hemingway. Hemingway, from 1925 to 1945, was almost *above* criticism. In 1937, following the publication of *To Have and Have Not*, a few of the more opportunistic critics began to take potshots at Ernie, intimating that he'd lost the old black magic. But Hemingway's *For Whom the Bell Tolls* followed quickly enough, and it made *so* much money as a movie, and Cooper and Bergman did *so* much to promote the sale of sleeping bags that the critics retired and bided their time. *To Have and Have Not* became a movie in the mid-Forties (at least the *title* was used) and Lauren Bacall again saved Hemingway's reputation for a time. But several more years passed and Hemingway produced nothing. The critics stuck their heads out of their holes (you are at liberty to interpret this figure of speech in any way that you wish, but please remember that the onus is on you, and I use the term advisedly) and began to nibble away at the Hemingway mantle. They discovered what discerning readers discovered years ago, at the height of the Hemingway Craze, that *Death in the Afternoon* is an amazing mish-mosh of high-level writing and sheer hokum; that *The Green Hills of Africa* is a journeyman job of travel trivia; that Mr. Hemingway wrote a singularly pedestrian series of fishing articles for *Esquire*; that his concept of Viscerotonic Man is not necessarily the Whole Truth Made Manifest.

And then Mr. Hemingway wrote *Across the River and Into the Trees* and they had their chance to pounce. For this was a bad book. It was a *very* bad book, and one of Mr. Hemingway's disciples, John O'Hara, made the mistake of praising it to the skies and comparing Hemingway favorably to the late Wm. Shakespeare, Esq. That did it. During the following year, Hemingway was the Number One Quintain for every Knight of the Pen.

(All right, *schmoe*, you can read about quintains in *The Sword in the Stone*, and it'll do you a damned sight more good than wasting your time over these ramblings, too.)

Hemingway, the critics wisely perceived, was a decadent, fascist-minded, sex-obsessed, egotistical, liquor-soaked has-been.

Then Mr. Hemingway sold several short stories to the movies. The resultant films (although hardly faithful representations) were highly successful at the box-office. Mr. Hemingway followed this up by selling *The Old Man and the Sea* to *Life* magazine for an unprecedented price, and an unprecedented printing in this picture-periodical. *The Old Man and the Sea* was a fine novella, and the aura of successful merchandising surrounding it did the trick.

The critics began to reverse themselves. Hemingway was the apostle of the positive — a yea-sayer with faith in the future, a true democratic spirit; mature, disciplined, humble, dedicated to his work.

When Mr. Hemingway followed up his book's appearance by a highly spectacular African plane crash, he became canonized and is now on the extreme edge of deification. The plane went down and Hemingway came up with an odor of sanctity.

The phenomenon I stress here, obviously, is that disparagement is not the only extreme which mars general critical judgment. Hysterical exaltation is also possible. The only thing that critics seem to suffer from as an occupational lack is objectivity.

Perhaps it is unfair for me to refer only to American writers in this respect: British examples abound. Witness the rise (and decline) of Rudyard Kipling; the rise (and decline — and gradual rise again) of W. Somerset Maugham; the rise (and decline, and slow evidence of incipient revival) of D.H. Lawrence and the rise and decline of Aldous Huxley. All these names have been showered with the most ecstatic, almost mystical praise — and damned to perdition by the same voices in subsequent years.

Now, at long last, against this background of critical vacillation, we come to the case of James Joyce and *Ulysses*.

There has always been a Joyce cult, even in the early days of *The Dubliners*. *The Portrait of an Artist as a Young Man* still has its vociferous admirers, and there are those who prefer the early-draft *Portrait* published as *Stephen Hero*, and those who dote upon *Finnegans Wake*.

But *Ulysses* is probably the book most closely identified with Joyce, and rightly so, for in it he posited and popularized (although he by no means invented) the form we all refer to as "stream of consciousness" writing.

Publication of *Ulysses*, as you probably know, was preceded and attended by stormy dissent. Smuggled portions of privately-printed text emerged from Paris. A court decision made the book available in the United States. All this made for publicity, and the big boom was on. Reading *Ulysses* was — for a time — as mandatory an obligation amongst self-styled intelligentsia as was an understanding of the Einstein Theory. That is to say, people *said* they had read *Ulysses*, just as they *said* they understood Einstein, and the critics plumped for it in the early Thirties just as they plumped for the Higher Art of Walt Disney, the Symbolic Value of Chaplin's little tramp, and the exaltation of the Poo over the Yobber.

The critics went to Night Town with Poldy and slid under the covers with Molly Bloom and a lovely time was had by all. Joyce, as might be expected by those who understand the critical temperament, was eulogized as the creator of a New Literature. Since *Ulysses* is not exactly easy reading there sprang up a variety of self-appointed "interpreters." These savants published articles and books to serve as "guides" or "keys" to the text, and some of these efforts made for amusement. I have seen it solemnly stated (and published) that Joyce wrote certain portions of the book in key with particular colors, in accord with certain astrological signs to govern his mood, etc. There was a definite effort to "annotate" Joyce as thoroughly as Shakespeare — with a paragraph of explanatory footnote for every word he wrote.

The inevitable result was that many potential readers, already dismayed by the apparent prolixity of Joyce's prose, were further discouraged by perusing one of these so-called "guides." And the critical huzzahs, blithely hailing Joyce as a Kindred Spirit to Gertrude Stein, Ezra Pound, and e e cummings, did nothing to reassure anyone.

I'd venture to say that Joyce lost a third of his audience because of his critical popularity; would-be *Ulysses* readers were frightened off by the sheer incoherence of the praise.

Then came the usual critical reaction. Joyce was "old hat," he hadn't *really* discovered "stream of consciousness" writing, he was actually just a "stream of self-consciousness" writer and the later *Finnegans Wake* was a "stream of subconscious" effort. Also Joyce was one of those smart-aleck Irishmen and (later) he didn't even *live* in Ireland, which proves that he was damned if he did and damned if he didn't, and besides it was possible to parody Joyce's style which proves something else again — viz, that he couldn't possibly be so much if he can be easily imitated by others.

So Joyce gradually lost favor with the critics, and thereby lost another third of his possible audience for *Ulysses*.

All of this has a special application in this particular instance, because *Ulysses* is a difficult book to read and to interpret; its sheer essence presents sufficient challenge to the average reader without the added heckling, pro and con, of critical reaction.

And yet *Ulysses* is an important book in that it has served, and served steadfastly over a score of years, as an inspirational springboard for many contemporary writers. Even Mr. Hemingway found it of use to him in portions of *To Have and Have Not*, as the discerning will discover, and many authors have not been ashamed to confess their indebtedness to Joyce in print.

Because of this phenomenon, some of Joyce's influence has come to be felt by indirection — I hazard that there are writers who have *not* read *Ulysses*, but *have* borrowed stylistic trappings discovered in the work of other writers who *were* copying Joyce.

To relate the matter to sf, almost every *Ulysses* reader will recognize the primal source of some of the *Esper* thought-and-conversation patterns in Bester's *The Demolished Man*, and in the frank stream-of-consciousness elements in Sturgeon's work (in which is also frequently adumbrated the relationship between Bloom and Stephen Dedalus). Novels such as Wolfe's *Limbo* owe much to Joyce's technique, and some of the devices which seem to startle the readers of *Galaxy* and *Astounding* can be easily traced to the world of Blazes Boylan and dear little Zoe.

There is no doubt but that Joyce's tortured humor caused him to embellish his account with the most elaborate puns and topical references to events and personages which we non-Dubliners, after a lapse of almost fifty years, find unintelligible. There is no doubt but that his wilfully involved style makes for hard going. There is no doubt but that his unannounced change of viewpoint, his trick of slipping from the conscious to the subconscious level in narration, offers a challenge to the reader.

But there is also, in my mind, no doubt but that the effort involved in a conscientious perusal of *Ulysses* is a rewarding one; no doubt but that the reader who addresses himself to the book will come away with full recognition of three memorable characters — Stephen Dedalus, Leopold Bloom and Molly Bloom.

And, more appositely, he will have, in the process, acquainted himself with the source of most of the so-called "modern" writing techniques which dazzle the naïve in general literature today as well as in sf.

Critical furor and fulmination aside, *Ulysses* towers head and shoulders above most twentieth century writing as a great source-book. Joyce well deserves a place beside Marcel Proust, Thomas Mann and that other eminent Irishman, Walter Kelly, for his contribution to lasting literature. If for no other reason than that he managed to drag so long and comparatively serious an essay out of me, Joyce will never be forgotten.

FROM HUBBUB HORIZONTAL

"Any man who cannot come to terms with the society in which he lives can call no one to blame but himself."

— John Brunner, *Nandu* #12

This strikes me as very naïve self-determinism indeed and full of semantic holes, and it is one point I wish had been more fully dealt with; i.e., what is meant by "come to terms?" and what constitutes "the society in which he lives?" and what is "blame?"

You could easily run a section on just this statement alone because it seems to prefigure, actually, an all-too-prevalent attitude today — viz: "I get along okay on this here basketball team because I'm six-foot-four. And if you five-foot-three guys can't get along, it's just your fault." This is the "philosophy" of *Time Magazine*, for example, with its constant stressing of our overall economic strength and its openly expressed scorn for social critics like Philip Wylie. This is, in effect, an expression of Wilson's "What's good for General Motors is good for the nation." It is what puts the GM prexy on the cover as *Time*'s Man of the Year: he made a billion dollars profit. And if he made a billion dollars profit for the company, then we all ought to be convinced that everything is dandy and it's up to us to go and do likewise — if we can't, it's *our* fault.

Without going off into any lengthy peroration, let me respectfully examine Brunner's statement and submit that:

(a) "Society" is a very loose concept, in that it is neither a homogeneous unit (clustering around General Motors, the Republican Party or — conversely — the mores of an Arkansas sharecropper community). Nor is it a static constant. It is a flux; an *abstract* flux at that, and any discussion of a "society" involves entering into a Spenglerian *mystique*.

(b) By "coming to terms" with that nebulous "society" I can only infer that Mr. Brunner is advocating "adjustment" or "conformity." This works out very well in ant colonies. On the human level, it's difficult for the individual — and suicidal for the group. Using the Brunner thesis, let's see what happens to an average citizen of the world — and just to shake ourselves out of our smug complacent attitude that the USA is the center of the known universe, let's select as our average citizen a Mr Johann Schmidt, age 60, of Berlin, Germany. How would Mr. Schmidt have fared in life if he adapted the Brunner dicta?

Mr. Schmidt, as a young man, would have adjusted by going around and *hoching der Kaiser*. In 1914 he would have dutifully joined the Imperial German Army and fought the Allies in defense of the German Empire. His personal "adjustment" during four years of war might well have included participation in looting, rape and murder — not because the Germans were necessarily such "beasts" but because it appears as if every army during time of war engages in such pastimes.

In the 1920s, Mr. Schmidt would have "adjusted" to the German Republic under men like Hindenburg. He might have become a Social Democrat or a National Socialist or a member of any of fifty different "parties" including the strong Communist bloc.

In the Thirties, Mr. (or, to give him his just due, Herr) Schmidt would, of course, have become a Nazi, a Hitlerite. From 1939 to 1945, he would have "adjusted" to torture, mass incineration, sabotage and all the rest of the practices his "society" not only condoned but conducted.

In 1945 and 1946, when the Allies occupied his native hearth, Herr Schmidt might well have "come to terms" with his society by protesting his innocence — he loved Democracy all along, but what could he do, etc.? Unless, of course, he happened to reside in the Russian Zone of Berlin, in which case — hooray for "coming to terms" — Schmidt would reveal that he had always been an ardent supporter of the Communist Party.

Good old blameless Herr Schmidt! *Sieg heil* for the man who can always "come to terms!" *Prosit* to the realistic thinker who does not quarrel or question current political, religious or ethical concepts!

Unfortunately, we're dealing with an abstraction here. My own notion is that a real-life Herr Schmidt wouldn't have reached any age 60. If he wasn't mowed down in his teens when the Kaiser's "society" told him to go out and face the machine guns, chances are he might well have starved to death in the succeeding decade when the Republican government was unable to control the ghastly inflation and subsequent depression. If he escaped that, his survival-potential during the Nazi years was slight enough: and if he goose-stepped for Hitler for six years, like his amiable fellow-conformists, it's almost inconceivable that he would survive such a further challenge of the laws of chance. My notion is that in reality, Herr Schmidt would be long gone dead.

Whereas a non-comer-to-terms, a complete questioner of his society, a man who refused to conform politically, religiously, ethically, and even questioned the basic scientific principles which guided it, could survive much more easily and efficiently. A man such as Herr Schmidt's one-time real-life fellow citizen, Albert Einstein.

No, this part of Mr. Brunner's belief I simply cannot buy. The individual is more important than the group, because when we examine the group we always find, basically, that it consists merely of a few top dogs and a lot of slaves. Call it Communism, Capitalism, Imperialism, what you will — a few govern and a lot of oafs conform and thus allow the few to exploit their own individuality at the expense of all the rest. Also, since "society" is an abstract, the whole business of "coming to terms" loses its validity — unless one is a complete hypocrite and opportunist like our hypothetical Schmidt. On the other hand, Mr. Brunner overlooks the fact that the individual, if he does not "come to terms," but goes his own way, can actually *change* this amorphous inconstant which he labels "society."

If you don't think so, I respectfully refer you to a little mathematical equation Einstein dreamed up which has had a pretty drastic effect on us all.

I do agree, however, with Mr. Brunner and most of the other essayists, that "genius" is no excuse for antisocial behavior, *per se*. On the other hand, we can't make the mistake of emphasizing one aspect of a personality and labelling it the whole. Mr. Brunner says, "the talent is not the owner." Neither, say I, is the character-flaw the owner — in Mr. Brunner's meaning of the phrase. A man can be a genius, a dope addict, a loving son, a domineering parent, a kind husband, a brutal exploiter of employees, a sensitive appreciator of music, an intolerant derider of graphic art, an enthusiastic baseball fan, a disinterested spectator of the political scene and a hundred other characters rolled into one. But no single facet *is* that person. Reducing our concept to "good geniuses" and "debauched geniuses" is a woeful oversimplification. And again, "good" and "bad" in the social or antisocial connotations of the terms, are changing concepts. The Greenes, Marlowes, Jonsons and Shakespeares of the Elizabethan era were probably not considered "antisocial" when they tippled nightly at the Mermaid: most of the gentlefolk and artists of that era indulged heavily in liquor. Cuckoldry and the taking of mistresses was widely condoned, except in the ranks of what were later to become the Dissenters and Roundheads. As for homosexuality, that too was rampant. On the other hand, free expression of opinion was definitely antisocial; it was, in a word, "treason," and immediately punishable by death.

Anyhow, I don't think we can characterize any "genius" fully in terms of his personal activities — any more than we can characterize the guy next door. My somewhat naïve notion is that most people (except for self-evident aberrees) respond pretty well to the Golden Rule. You're nice to them, they're nice to you. And as far as I'm personally concerned, that's all I have a right to ask of them — that their relations with me be mutually pleasant. I cannot control their behavior patterns, nor have I the right to either impose control or even pretend to *judge* them by my own so-called "standards." As for "coming to terms," I think every adjustment problem must necessarily be considered on the individual level, in reality.

THE LOMOKOME PAPERS

In February, 1956, *Collier's* printed "a brilliant social and political satire — fantastic adventures of the first man to pilot a rocket to the moon." It was "The Lomokome Papers," by Herman Wouk, a masterpiece of sf and satire from its clever opening words, ". . . forgotten a lot already" to its brilliant concluding sentence, "no more time." If you remember the excellent critical reviews by Robert Bloch in the old *Arkham Samplers* then you will understand why it is with such delight that we present his comments on "The Lomokome Papers" which supposedly netted Wouk a dollar a word. Is there any wonder now, why *Collier's* has ceased publication?

— Jerry DeMuth

I approached "The Lomokome Papers" with high hopes. To begin with I am always delighted when an sf or fantasy yarn finds a place for itself in a big, general-circulation magazine. I think it's good advertising for the field and can help attract readers. Secondly, the fact that the story was by Herman Wouk carried a certain amount of general prestige value. Wouk has made a big name for himself and a big buck. Ordinary readers unacquainted with sf might be impressed by the fact that a man like Wouk would choose to write in the medium.

When *Collier's* ran the story they even went so far as to put a picture of Herman Wouk on the cover, in full color yet. In the background, seated at a desk and staring right at the reader, was our boy Herman in the pose of a deep thinker straight. In case you never saw this cover, he looked something like Bill Hamling sitting down and starting to think up an editorial.

Well, I admit, this cover bothered me a little. Then, when I turned to the inside pages and discovered those little notes about authors, I read that "The Lomokome Papers" wasn't exactly a *new* effort. It seems the manuscript had been lying around unpublished for quite a few years. But one day when Herman was cleaning house, he discovered it someplace — lining the bottom of a birdcage, or something like that. And he sort of tidied it up a bit and sent it out, and *Collier's* was delighted because here was a real gem.

By the time I finished reading this, I was perhaps a trifle hesitant. I know how quickly a bestselling author can start palming off his old rejects on editors. One has only to stop and remember how, after selling *The Chinese Doll*, Wilson Tucker was able to unload about twelve more dud books on the unsuspecting publishers. But on the other hand, I reasoned, maybe Wouk's story had been unpublished previously merely because it *was* sf and the editors had a prejudice against it. So I read "The Lomokome Papers."

Now I am not by any means a model citizen. I may very easily, at some future date, commit some crime or misdemeanor. I may get into a lot of trouble and perhaps be punished and ostracized. But if that ever happens, and you have any reason to condemn me, all I ask of you is one thing. Please stop and remember that I read "The Lomokome Papers." And no matter what I do, this has been punishment enough.

I have read bad books in my time. I have read hack-work and slop and crudzines, and even some issues of *Destiny*. But I have never, I repeat, *never* read anything that pretended to be so much and was so little as "The Lomokome Papers."

That's the point, if any. It isn't that one could not find *worse* sf, word-for-word, if one wanted to browse through old pulps of the 1920s and come up with some horrible examples of bem and mad scientist yarns. But few of these ancient pulp thrillers made any pretensions of being anything else than just that. On the other hand, here is one of America's top-name authors, sitting on the cover and thinking right at you in four colors with a masterpiece. Well, "The Lomokome Papers" is a masterpiece, all right . . . but I'd hesitate to say what it is a masterpiece *of*. To be mercifully brief, the story runs . . . or rather crawls . . . something like this.

It starts with an introductory section in the form of an "official report" from the Navy . . . to the effect that in 1954 two manned projectiles reached the moon. The first crashed there, carrying a Lieutenant Butler who narrates the actual story which follows. The second returned, after trying to find Butler and locating one hundred and seven sheets of notes in Butler's handwriting. These series of notes make up "The Lomokome Papers."

As is usual in these yarns — you have read them a hundred times and so, apparently, has Herman Wouk — the so-called report claims to disbelieve the story — and the story itself is supposed to convince the reader that it's true anyway. This is a great, little, original gimmick, isn't it? Unless you happen to have read H. P. Lovecraft twenty-five years ago or H.G. Wells fifty years ago.

The "report" implies that Lt. Butler, the narrator of the story, was writing after falling into a crater and using up his oxygen supply, and that he was delirious. Then Wouk goes into the story and tries to prove his narrator was delirious.

The so-called story in note form begins very conveniently in mid-air. Butler has arrived on the moon. (Wouk never tells us how he got there, and thus doesn't have to bother making it convincing.) Butler has met the natives (again we are never told how) and has made friends with them (we are never told how) and has somehow been taught their language. These natives — now get this — live in caves under the moon's surface. There's a jim-dandy original idea, isn't it? I wonder how long you would have to sit with hand on forehead before you could think up a novel notion like this!

Wait, there's more to come. Our hero lives with a wise old scientist named Vove, and his beautiful daughter, Vovone. How about that, now? A wise old scientist and his beautiful daughter. And — dig this, cats — their skin is *green*! So help me, it's green! Moon-people with green skin. This guy Herman is what I call a real original-thinker type genius.

Well, after another break in the narrative — so Herman could do more thinking with his finger on his forehead or somewhere — we get another bit. The moon people live in caves illuminated by orange light and they wear orange robes and they have a big Central Cavern to meet in. Herman doesn't say if they have bug eyes or not — but outside of that he doesn't miss a trick. Except, perhaps, to explain things through extrapolation. We do learn that the hero has been taught the language, and is a guest, and that these people "pipe sunlight into their homes as we pipe water" — that's a direct quote so don't blame me — and use a system of reflector relays. Presumably straight out of an old *Tom Swift* book.

We also learn that these Lomokians are actually colonists from — oops, can't tell you that, because Author Wouk breaks off his narrative again here. Too much work trying to figure out where his humanoid lunarians come from.

When he resumes his story the scientist Vove has been arrested, and the hero lives somewhere else. Wouk now rambles on about the two moon nations, the Lomokome and the Lomadine, and their history. They fought a lot of wars with a fissionable nitrogen cloud as a weapon. The Lomokome government is based on a social system of Hydrogenism and the Lomadine order is based on

Suggestionism. These systems are briefly described but never developed.

Then come some excerpts from the Book of Ctuzelawis, the wise man who invented the Law of Reasonable War. This quotation, in pseudo-Biblical language, is a satire, a statement on how to wage war without destroying a nation. And it is pretty good stuff, too, what there is of it, about the equivalent of a lengthy satirical article such as you might find in a serious constructive fanzine such as Fritz Leiber's *New Purposes*. Indirectly, by reading it, we discover why the scientist Vove must die on Death Day — as a leader of his people selected as a martyr.

Then comes another fragment and we learn that Vovone, his beautiful daughter, and the narrator plan to escape Death Day and get to the crashed projectile nine hundred miles away on the moon's surface. They do this in the next fragment without all of that messy business of plotting and action and dialogue that clutters up the average story — they just plain do it, in some kind of machine. No trouble at all.

And in the next fragment they are apparently captured while trying to repair the projectile and there the narrative ends.

Very simple. But my question is: how simple can you get? A word about that satire on war, now. I've already heard several people compare it to the work of Jonathan Swift. Unfortunately, the comparison just doesn't hold. Consider *Gulliver's Travels* for a moment. There is a book — in fact, four books. In them, Swift tells a story, a real story, so real that it still stands up today in narrative form, or in an adaptation for children without the satirical element. And the satirical element itself is carefully woven into a plot. There is actual characterization present.

Whereas in "The Lomokome Papers" we find nothing but a satirical section encapsulated in one of the poorest excuses for a story ever presented. Every time Wouk has to face a problem of Who, What, Where, or Why — problems which are faced daily and must be faced by any hack writer who wants to sell for a half cent a word market — he merely ducks the issue by breaking off his "fragment." His so-called setting and so-called characters are borrowed from the most ancient pulps and there isn't the slightest effort made at actual description or actual characterization.

This is lazy man's writing. I contend that "The Lomokome Papers" is not a novel, not a novelette — merely a disorganized jumble that couldn't sell to the worst market in the field if it didn't have a big name attached to it.

Now maybe this is envy, it might well be. But by any critical standards, there's absolutely no excuse for this thing except the satirical element. And that is poorly injected. Worse, I don't even believe it's honest. Wouk, in the

Collier's "notes," is reported as saying he originally planned to write a play about the Bomb, which appeared in 1949 in New York and — although Wouk doesn't mention it — failed. Probably a case of all Wouk and no play. He then took the same idea, developed it as a fantasy, but — he says — put it aside because the Korean War came along and he did not want to put out any anti-war stuff because he happened to "believe" in the Korean War. So here's a guy writing a satire which has no reason or excuse for existence except its anti-war sentiment — and he sets it aside because a war comes along and he "believes" in the war. Maybe I'm dense, but I just don't get this kind of double-thinking. And it certainly destroys the "value" of the satire for me.

But to me the worst crime of all, as it applies to the sf field, is that Wouk has wittingly or unwittingly smeared us again. A straight sf story appears only on rare occasions in a big general magazine like *Collier's*. When it does, presumably it will be read by several million people who don't generally read sf. If it's a good job, it might well serve to interest a lot of potential readers in the field. And when it bears a big name — like Wouk's — it presumably represents "the best" of its kind to readers unfamiliar with sf. In this case, I'd venture to say that a good three-fourths of the *Collier's* readers never got beyond the second page of "The Lomokome Papers" before throwing it down and reaching for the TV dial. The muddled writing, the tedious passages, the hackneyed concepts, the pretentious and self-conscious style probably discouraged them completely. "If THIS is what sf is supposed to be — if one of the biggest best-selling writers in the country can't make it any more interesting than THAT — then I sure ain't gonna read no more sf no-how." That's the kind of reader reaction "The Lomokome Papers" would generally inspire. Not only does it discourage the printing of further sf material in general magazines — it also keeps potential readers away from the regular sf magazines themselves.

The anti-war satire, while clever in itself, is no excuse for the sloppy, rambling format which passes as a "novel." Presented as a straight short essay, it could find a logical place in magazine pages. But it doesn't belong in a so-called narrative of this sort any more than it belongs in *Marjorie Morningstar*.

The contrast between this work and something like *1984* can be measured only in astronomical figures. Let's take some of the elements which I personally think are necessary for good sf and see how the two books stack up in terms of them.

First of all, credibility. It's my notion that you simply cannot have a good sf story without credibility. Granted that the reader must bring to his reading what Coleridge calls "the willing suspension of disbelief," it's still up to the author to help him — even in so-called "mainstream literature." If the sf writer doesn't give his work credibility, the result is not sf but fantasy. And even there, the best fantasy makes an effort to be convincing — or at least logical within its established frame of reference.

In terms of credibility, *1984* is a masterful job. You may not like the picture of the world that Orwell paints, but he shows it to you in convincing detail.

As for "The Lomokome Papers," here we find no attempt made to convince the reader — except the trite old gag about pretending the story is a part of an official report. Even if we accept this tired premise, the result is wholly unconvincing. The narrator is on the moon presumably as a Navy observer on active duty. Does he take notes on what he sees — describe the flora, the fauna, the topography, the atmosphere? Does he sound like a man on official business interested in the moon as a potential military base or colony? Does he speak of the inhabitants in terms of their actions and reactions, their relationship to human or known life-forms? Not a bit. He is a most unconvincing and unlikely narrator. And of course, the events he does narrate are equally sketchy and unconvincing. There is little or no motivation offered for anything that happens.

Now, we come to characterization. Again, it is an important element — except in a few cases where sf is offered as pseudo-history, as is the case of Arthur C. Clarke's *Childhood's End* or Stapledon's *Last and First Men*. But in a story involving a protagonist and his relationships with others, it's very definitely necessary to get to know that protagonist and to know something about the people who are allied with him or oppose him. In *1984*, Orwell has given a vivid picture of Winston Smith — or of O'Brien, and of Julia. And he's done it in the third person. In "The Lomokome Papers," Wouk has chosen a first person narration — an even more intimate method of giving the reader an insight into the thoughts and personality of the hero. What do we learn about Lieutenant Butler? Absolutely nothing, except his name. There isn't the faintest clue as to what type of a man he is, or why he behaves as he does. In one paragraph, describing the girl Vovone, he admits he likes the athletic type of female — and that's all. Similarly, we don't find out anything about the wise old scientist or his charming daughter. The cruddiest comic book at least attempts to give the reader some stereotype as a substitute for individual characterization. Wouk gives nothing. There is no reason for the reader to identify with anyone in the story, no reason for him to care what happens. Maybe this is a good thing, because not too much happens.

Now we come to continuity. By this I mean the construction of the story — the plot, the storyline. In *1984*, the story is so well integrated with the theme that its emergence seems almost inevitable, step by step. Everything ties in, cause is followed by effect. In "The Lomokome Papers," there's just a fragmentary mishmash — any time Wouk has to face the problem of a plot, any time he has to present action or reaction, he just ducks it and rambles on into another episode. He backtracks amateurishly again and again to explain how he happens to be writing something which has no relationship with what went before. And he thereby cheats the reader.

Finally, there is creativity. That is to say, the imaginative, evocative element every writer must put into his work to make it distinctive, individual, significant — even when you water these terms down to apply them to pulp work. This is the vital spark. In *1984*, creativity consists of vividly portraying a whole extrapolated civilization, logically tracing the development of certain totalitarian tendencies to their inevitable conclusion, granted the necessary circumstances. The whole idea of Big Brother, of the double-think world complete with ideology and vocabulary stems from Orwell's creativity. What does Wouk's creativity give us? The wise old scientist and his daughter — with green skins — living in caverns under the moon. Period. Plus his satire. The difference between Orwell's satire and Wouk's is that Orwell made a book out of it and Wouk just makes a satire sandwich — a little hunk of meat between two of the stalest and mouldiest pieces of crummy old bread that were ever baked in the Gernsback ovens of 1926.

By the way, it's perhaps interesting to note two things regarding Wouk's work as a whole. One critic, in discussing *1984*, tried to relate Orwell's work to his actual personal psychology. I've never seen this attempted with Wouk, but I'd like to take a crack at it. If we ignore *Aurora Dawn* and *City Boy*, his early efforts, and concentrate on his popular successes, *The Caine Mutiny* and *Marjorie Morningstar*, it's at once self-evident that Wouk has two fixed beliefs: (1) So-called "intellectuals" are no damned good and (2) the Law is the real Authority. In *The Caine Mutiny*, you may remember, the villain is not Queeg but the book-writing lieutenant who stirs up the trouble. And the lawyer who wins the trial and saves Willie Keith is the real hero who at the end vindicates Queeg and the Navy, not because they are necessarily "right" but because both Queeg's actions as captain and the Navy's rulings regarding mutiny are a part of established law.

In *Marjorie Morningstar*, we find the villain, Noel Airman, is another one of those nasty "intellectual" types — which, according to the way Wouk likes to load his argument, are always weaklings and poseurs. And Marjorie ends up by marrying (of all things) a lawyer. Meanwhile, her mother lays down the law to her and there is a general attempt throughout the book to posit the notion that the "moral law" and the religious "laws" of Judaism are Authority.

At first glance it is hard to see this pattern, punishment for the so-called "intellectual" and veneration for the so-called "law," in the fumbled confusion of "The Lomokome Papers." Until we suddenly realize that the whole thing is merely a crude restatement of the old Wouk theme. The narrator of the book is himself a *writer.* He is officially branded by the Navy report in the foreword as a crazy, mixed-up kid and he presumably is destroyed in the end. And the heart of the book, the satire on war is bluntly presented as *The Law* of Reasonable War. So here it is again and it raises the question what happened to Herman Wouk that makes him so bitter against so-called "intellectuals" and what makes him so determined to uphold the *status quo* in the form of "laws" and religious codes? It's an interesting question.

A NON-LEWIS CAROL

"You are old, Author William," the neofan said
    "And your hair has become very white;
And yet at conventions you're never abed —
    Do you think, at your age, it is right?"

"In my youth," Author William replied to the fan
    "Reputation I feared it might stain;
But now that I'm perfectly sure I have none,
    Why, I stay up again and again."

"You are old," said the fan, "as I mentioned before
    And your writing is surely quite flat.
Yet you said in your con-speech your yarns appear more.
    Pray what is the reason for that?"

"In my youth," said the pro, "My stories were fine,
    And they all stayed unsold on the shelf.
Now I plagiarize Bradbury, Clarke and Heinlein —
    But I edit a prozine myself."

"You are old," said the fan, "and your hands are too weak
    To type any more than a page;
Yet you fling water-bags out as fast as a streak —
    Pray, how is that, at your age?"

"In my youth," said the pro, "I played poker with dubs
    At conventions for days without dropping,
And palming the aces or the Ten of Clubs
    Gave me strength to play pranks without stopping."

"You are old," said the fan "and you drink like a fish;
Yet con-parties you attend at random.
Omnipresent as Harmon, Ellison or Ish —
Can it be you're in Seventh Fandom?"

"I have answered three questions, and that is enough
— You're like Tucker, with his questionnaires!
Now be off," said the pro, "for I'm sick of this stuff!
Besides, I've a date with the Shares."

CASSANDRA

I remember the prophets without honor
And how they used to skulk down alleys,
Hiding the magazines under their coats,
Ripping off the lurid covers,
Apologizing softly for their reading taste
Until the wine ran defiant in their veins.
Then: "The day will come," they said.
"The day will come, and surely, when we prevail,
Our tastes, our dicta reign supreme."
They gnawed stale bread and their wine was poor
(What can you buy for half-a-cent a word?)
But never faltered in their faith.
Their eyes were bright upon the future.
They spoke of brave new worlds and things to come
And dreamed of sainthood in the latter day.
Well, they spoke truly. Look about and see.
It's all yours, upon a silver platter.
The literary critics bless, the readers buy,
The editors and publishers defer.
Trimmed edges? So be it, as ye wish.
Artistic covers, permanently glazed?
Why not? All this and increased wordage too.
Let all the world take note of our reviews;

(continued)

The leading journals of opinion honor us
And Hollywood lends three dimensions in glorious Technicolor.
Book-of-the-month, television, foreign rights,
Royalties, bonuses, pocket-book assured,
Contests, awards, banquets, adoration
And the accolade of luncheon at the Stork.
It's here, it's not a dream, it's true!
The prophets are not without profits today
And there's talk of further boom and further fields
Of influence subtly wielded,
Opinion deftly molded,
Why should we stop at this?
Go on now — lead the way
They wrote of nuclear fission and it came to pass.
They postulate new science of the mind
They need not falter: Keep it up!
Predict new government, technological, authoritarian,
And who knows where it all can end?
Perhaps the alleys lead to final thrones!
Write on, dream on, speed the day.
But wait — one final prophecy!
Ere Science and its minions reign supreme
And smugly mark Millennium's approach.
Cock an ear. Do you detect a distant sound?
A bang? A whimper?
I skulk down alleys, but I hear it now. . . .

JABBERWOCKY FOR FANDOM

'Twas Willis, and the boggsy toves
  Did gold and campbell in the wabe:
All faunchy were the borogoves
  And the Seventh Fans outgrabe.

Beware the Fannishtalk, my son!
    The paws that write, the feuds that catch!
Beware the FAPA bird, and shun
    Both GRUE and HYPHEN, natch!

He took his hectograph in hand:
    Long time the poctsarcd foe he sought —
So rested by the Annish tree,
    And stood awhile in thought.

And as in tuckerish thought he stood,
    The Fannishtalk, with eyes of flame,
Came yngving through the lousy wood,
    And burbeed as it came!

One, two! One, two! And through and through
    The vorpal blade sawed Courtney's boat!
His pen hit snags of fannish gags
    As he, little willies wrote.

    "And hast thou learned the Fannishtalk?
    Come to my arms, my harlan boy!
    Oh Poo, Oh Yobber, Ghu, horray!"
    He grennelled in his joy.

    'Twas harris, and the laney toves
    Did f&sf in the wabe,
    All crifanac the borogoves
    As in gafia he outgrabe.

ONE SMALL ANECDOTE STARRING R. BLOCH AND H. ELLISON

by Harlan Ellison

Of his endless kindness you've heard pæans. Litanies of the stories that shaped and enriched half a dozen genres are pandemic. What he said at this convention, what he did at that roast . . . passed into legend. It seems he has always been with us; and the world of fantastic literature is inconceivable without him. He is a nexus. There are those who judge their worth in this life by the sole fact that he is their friend.

How many times I've been asked to write "just a few words of appreciation" of Bob Bloch! And no matter how many trips to that well, there is always one more bucketful of whimsy to pull up. Here's one of the most bizarre.

Dreams. How we live in them. How they make the days of keeping appointments, of drudgework, of spending time in the company of people who say things we've heard, in just those same words, a thousand times . . . just a little more bearable. Without them, what an utter desolation of predictability and frustration. Bloch knows this. He's spent most of his life spading up those potato dreams, mashing and serving them with a

---

In a much-abbreviated form, this essay appeared in *The Harlan Ellison Hornbook* (Mirage Press, Penzler Books, 1990). It has been specially expanded and rewritten at twice its original length.

rich country gravy of mischievous wickedness. He knows that without the dreams, the suicide stats would be cataclysmic.

And yet, the best dreams of all are not the ones we carry with us for years; or the ones that come true; or the ones that stay always just out of reach. The best dreams are the ones that come upon us suddenly, startling us like Bambi in the forest.

The ones we never knew we had, till we're suddenly living them. I'll tell you one that happened to Bloch and me.

We've been lots of places together. Ohio, New York, even exotic Milwaukee. But the most interesting trip we ever took was to Brazil. Rio in the primeval blistering cauldron of March 1969. A country ruled ruthlessly by a military *junta* that decorated the street corners every night with tanks and machine gun emplacements. To Rio journeyed Bloch and Ellison.

The Trylon and Perisphere of the realm phantasmagoric.

It was 1969. Bob and I had been invited — along with such luminaries as Agnes Varda, Roman Polanski, Josef von Sternberg, Roger Corman, and Diane Varsi — as well as a gaggle of fantasists that included Heinlein, Bester, Harrison, Sheckley, Van Vogt, and Farmer — to be guests of the 2nd International Film Festival of Rio de Janeiro. Despite the depressing realities of life in that glittering, jungle-bordered metropolis baking in the lee of Sugar Loaf — for the abyss that lies between the obscenely wealthy and the grindingly poor in Brazil is a thousand times more pronounced and heartbreaking than here in the States — being treated like princes from a far land took our breath away.

And the dream came to Bob and me like this:

As "notables" we received invitations to endless embassy receptions. Rio had lost its senses and gone ga-ga over this contingent of famous film and fantasy folk. Everywhere we went we were cheered as though we had somehow contributed to the advancement of Western Culture when, in fact, we were only a *divertissement* for the Leblon billionaires. We were that hot season's incarnation of bread and circuses. Bloch was the bread; I was the chicken fat.

Have I mentioned the women? Oh, my friends, the women of Rio! Gleaming black sweeps of hair hanging to the small of their backs. Toasted a thousand shades of golden treasure. In the day, barely clothed as they languished on the beaches; by night, whispering in white silk at the embassy parties. Oh, my friends, the forbidden conversations Bloch and I shared!

But after the first three or four of such social orgies, staged with incredible opulence in settings of art and grandeur (and very quickly painful to me, when matched against the awful sights that burned in my mind: the *peons* in their hillside *favellas*, feeding a dozen family members, children, animals, from one big kettle in the front "yard" of their tin-roofed hovels . . . going without food so they could buy candles to burn on the balustrades of the thousand-step stoneways that climb to the glorious Catholic cathedrals . . . the young women wearing themselves down to premature middle-age working in the factories so their shark-thin young men have the free time to hustle wealthy American and German tourist widows on the Copacabana beach), I found myself being sickened by the profligacy. Both Bob and I resolved to attend no more of these charades.

Yet our hideous sense of gallows humor compelled us to make one special exception. We had received an invitation to the reception at the Polish embassy. This was 1969, remember.

We confess to an ugliness of nature that demanded we see what the Polish embassy was like.

We were advised it was black tie, and that we should assemble in front of our hotel at 5:00 to be transported by limousines. It was 120 in Rio that summer, and even the joke that passed for air conditioning in the hotel was suffering from Cheyne-Stokes respiration. So at quarter to five we found ourselves decked out in elegance (Bloch looks *smashing* in a tux), standing on the restaurant patio, waiting for the limos that had been promised.

In Rio, time comes slathered with molasses. When they say 5:00 they mean 5:30 if you're lucky; 6:00 if they're on time; 6:30 if they're running true to form; and 7:00 if they're a little behind schedule. By 7:30 we were drenched and redolent, thoroughly wilted and swimming in our tuxedos. And finally the "limousines" arrived: four old and incredibly swaybacked buses.

Soggily, we climbed aboard, like brutalized *mestizos* being chivvied back to the castor-bean plantations for another fifteen hours of backbreaking labor under that assassin oven, the open sky. Shortly after 8:00 we rolled out to the Polish embassy.

Understand this: in Rio the embassies outdo one another for sumptuousness. The Spanish Embassy is in a renovated villa, festooned with ancient tapestries, reeking of history and *Droit du Seigneur*. Harry Harrison told me about it. He went, I didn't. The American reception was held in an art museum, with three rock bands, light shows, and old movies flashed on the walls, champagne flowing, beluga and osetra in tureens filled to surface tension, all free-form and glass walls. One could expect no less from the Polish Embassy. Unless, like Bloch and Ellison, one had a gallows sense of humor.

The Polish Embassy was like a bad Polack joke. It was on the third floor (walk-up) of a nondescript apartment building: a huge, empty series of rooms utterly devoid of furniture. No air conditioning. No music. No chairs, we stood or leaned. The refreshments seemingly consisted solely of cornucopial flowings of *slivovitz* and an extraterrestrially mutated species of *vodka* Brian Aldiss assured me could be used to launch a Soyuz rocket into Lunar orbit. (Not being a drinker, I have to rely on the opinions of experts in these matters.)

As the humidity was 100% and the heat was bubbling well over a hundred degrees, with everyone schvitzing like malamutes, within an hour the crowded "embassy" was ass-deep in drunken dignitaries, babbling at one another in a dozen tongues, making no sense, sweat-stinking and jammed belly-to-backside like slaves in the hold of a privateer, everyone demented as fruit-bats and beginning to look like characters out of one of Bloch's most hallucinogenic stories.

Bob and I clung together for protection like a couple of Spartans at the Hot Gates. Like Eliza and Little Eva on an ice floe. Like the last two survivors at Fort Zinderneuf.

The Polish attachés were, how shall I put it, *sensational*! To a man they were all squat, hemispherical, cherubic, and clad in heavy wool suits (with vests) that may well have been out of fashion even when they were soldered together in 1938. Miraculously, even in the oily, dripping atmosphere of that gulag apartment, vacuum-packed with several hundred gibbering eye-rolling aliens, our own little dungeon of Babel, with droplets of moisture condensing on the walls 'neath a stillatitious ceiling . . . even in those grotesque woolen suits . . . not one of them perspired!

Bob and I wandered around the empty rooms looking for a couple of feet of untenanted space where we could draw a breath of air that hadn't been recycled through laboring lungs. We found our way into what might have been the living room, had it contained even a stick of furniture. And it was there that the dream took root.

As we came into that huge, empty space, we found our eyes drawn to the only non-human item in the room. (Or perhaps we were hasty in our judgment of some affinity with humanity, non- or otherwise.) There was an enormous painting on the wall. Bob looked at it; I looked at it; then we looked at each other. Bob shivered. I felt a centipede traverse my spine.

"Does that look to you like what it looks like to me?" I asked. Bob nodded. He *kept* nodding; like he couldn't stop; as if he were having a seizure.

The painting was a hideous green and yellow smash of unparalleled ghastliness. Disreputably alien, disturbingly suggestive, distressingly nauseating, it looked like some soft wet thing fallen out of a Lovecraft nightmare. Something unnameable and unspeakable, one of those Elder Gods, with a name like Yog-Sothoth, or maybe Yig, or at least a close relative that not even the rest of that icky family would acknowledge. This was genuine puke art. Bloch was now mumbling.

I took him by the elbow as his eyes glazed over and, shuddering, we turned away; and neither of us strayed back into that room during the entire reception. We pressed our way swiftly, perhaps a trifle hysterically, into the farthest corner of the farthest room from that portrait, what might have been the "dining room," trying with equal vigor to get as far away from the nasty thing as we could, while positioning ourselves next to the one open window in the apartment.

Now the dream comes to full flower.

I tell it *precisely* as it happened, sans comment, sans embellishment. This one needs no flourishes; it is true. You can ask Bloch. Sure, *I* lie, but everyone knows Bloch is a pillar of rectitude.

I was looking out the window, mired in sweat and ennui, tasting the spice of oblivion, when my eyes traveled across the narrow street to the apartment building directly opposite. One floor above us, across the way, the curtains were parted, revealing the interior of an apartment. Windows wide open in hopes of a vagrant cooling breeze. Absolute clarity of view. I stared into that apartment for almost a minute before my brain would accept what I was seeing:

On the wall was an enormous blood-red flag with the Nazi swastika emblazoned in the center in glossy black, as if it had been painted with laquer over the original print. The flag was torn and frayed at the edges, as if it had possibly been ripped, suddenly, from the wall of a building going up in flames. But perhaps I dramatize. It may just have been old and weathered.

On another wall, there was a huge, framed photograph of

Adolf Hitler.

And marching back and forth in front of the window was a gentleman whose face I could not see, dressed in the black leather and livery of an SS *Oberstgruppenfüehrer*. He was marching stiffly, as if his limberness had decreased with age, in what newsreels have always advised me was a "goose-step."

I stared, dumbfounded, for a couple of minutes. Deep in the dream. Suffocating in the nightmare. Then, in that time-lapse state of dreaming, I slowly reached over and touched Bob's hand. "Take a look, that apartment across the street. Tell me if I'm seeing what I think I'm seeing, Bob."

He bent around me and looked. He was silent for some time. Then he looked around at me and tried several times to say something. When he finally got it out, it was a breathy kind of "Oh my god."

We stood silently, side by side, and just stared.

After a while, we called several other people's attention to the tableau; and they all seemed chilled by the sight. But they all saw it. Not too long after, the fellow in the other apartment saw us staring, and he pulled the curtains closed.

Further, deponent sayeth not; save to comment that this was, remember, 1969. It had been less than ten years since an agent of the Israeli Mossad had walked up to Adolf Eichmann, thirty years a fugitive of Holocaust justice, on Garibaldi Street in Buenos Aires, and said, "*Un momentito, señor.*" Mengele, Müller, and Martin Bormann were still out there, rumored to be living comfortably in Venezuela, Argentina, Ecuador. We knew nothing of Kurt Waldheim's odious past. We could not have suspected that the vile Klaus Barbie, "the butcher of Lyon," had been provided escape, succor, and decades-long cover by Western intelligence agencies.

Bob Bloch had written of realized horrors unceasingly for years; but now he stood staring wordlessly as the dream that was pure nightmare produced its rotting blossoms. We have spoken often of the aroma of fear and evil that permeated the ludicrous Polish "embassy" that evening in Rio de Janeiro. And of all the moments I might have recounted by way of "appreciation," this has been the one that most deeply touched us not only as friends, not only as fellow writers, but as part of the human wad that never ever really escapes the terrors that are of our own making.

www.ingramcontent.com/pod-product-compliance
Lightning Source LLC
Chambersburg PA
CBHW030811310726
48980CB00006B/459/J
9781880448168